Visual
Forces

Visual Forces

An Introduction to Design

BENJAMIN MARTINEZ

JACQUELINE BLOCK

PRENTICE HALL
ENGLEWOOD CLIFFS, NEW JERSEY 07632

Library of Congress Cataloging-in-Publication Data

Martinez, Benjamin (date)
    Visual forces.

    Bibliography:
    Includes index.
    1. Composition (art) 2. Design. I. Block,
Jacqueline (date). II. Title.
N7430.M294 1988   701'.8   87-19308
ISBN 0-13-942590-X

Editorial/production supervision: F. Hubert
Cover design: Peggy Finnerty
Manufacturing buyer: Ray Keating
Cover art: Juan Gris, ''Fantomas.''
Dated 1915. (National Gallery of Art,
Washington, D.C.; Chester Dale Fund, 1976)

Printed in the United States of America

10 9 8 7 6 5 4 3 2

ISBN 0-13-942590-X 01

Prentice-Hall International (UK) Limited, *London*
Prentice-Hall of Australia Pty. Limited, *Sydney*
Prentice-Hall Canada Inc., *Toronto*
Prentice-Hall Hispanoamericana, S.A., *Mexico*
Prentice-Hall of India Private Limited, *New Delhi*
Prentice-Hall of Japan, Inc., *Tokyo*
Simon & Schuster Asia Pte. Ltd., *Singapore*
Editora Prentice-Hall do Brasil, Ltda., *Rio de Janeiro*

Contents

CONTENTS

Preface

This could be called a book about basic design. Since *all* serious study in the arts is about basics, however, no matter how "advanced" or refined the materials or the techniques, the questions and possibilities dealt with here are those dealt with by the experienced visual artist as well as by the art student.

Each of the eleven chapters covers a different general area, but the topics to some extent resist being completely compartmentalized. It is difficult to talk about perspective, for example, without talking about flatness or pictorial space.

We have dealt with this problem in two ways. First, the units within each chapter *do* lead from one to another in a logical way. Each unit is buttressed by relevant information in the units immediately before and after it. The overall arrangement of the book is also a logical one (although we considered other, equally logical plans), and we *do* suggest that any user read at least the first four chapters in order. The book can also be used as a design "dictionary," a stockpile of extended definitions to be referred to in any order.

Second, we have used a simple cross-referencing system, unique to design texts. At the end of almost every unit is a listing of from one to five other units where you will find related information, either in other parts of the book or in the same chapter.

No book of this kind can cover every aspect of the subject, and a bibliography is included as a guide to other useful books in the field. We feel that, for both the information contained and for the organization of concepts, this is a book that will earn its keep.

Benjamin Martinez
Jacqueline Block

Visual
Forces

El Lissitzky, ''Beat the Whites with the Red Wedge.'' 1919.
(Stedelijk van Abbemuseum, Eindhoven, the Netherlands)

Introduction

1

Relationships

IN discussions of visual art, the word *relation-ship* is one that is used so frequently that it is worth our taking a moment at the start to define the term.

In everyday usage, a relationship is some type of connection between people or things. For example, members of a family are connected by either blood or marriage. Although there may be some physical resemblance between family members, this type of relationship is generally one that we understand conceptually, rather than visually. In art and design, on the other hand, relationships are basically *visual* connections—between one shape and another, between a shape and a line, between a group of color spots and the edge of the page. This connection can be literal or not. You might connect two shapes by actually drawing a line from one to the other. Usually, however, the connections we perceive are more subtle.

For instance, we could say that one shape is higher up on a page than another, or that one is further from the bottom edge of the page than the other. Such a connection—one that is invisible in one sense, but also easy to see—is related to comparing distances or intervals between things.

In fact, everything we see is seen by comparing. Your hair may be dark compared with your friend's, or light compared with the color of the chair you're sitting on. A plum is not very round compared with an orange, but it does seem round when compared with a potato. Similarly, we establish that a shape in a design is tilted at an angle by comparing it with the edge of the page.

In other words, we understand the different qualities of a given form in context, by seeing it in relation to its neighbors, and the appearance of a shape, a color, or other characteristic is affected by these relationships.

The other aspect of relationship that concerns us is the sense of the larger whole. You and an uncle, for example, are connected in both being part of a larger family, in which you each have a different role. In a work of art, there are different shapes, colors, and textures, but put together, they create a whole visual event that is different from all the bits and pieces.

All of these qualities—connecting, being compared, and relating to each other to create a visual whole—are the materials artists work with as much as they do with pencils or oil paint or circles and squares. Works of art consist of relationships between forms as much as the forms themselves.

Families of Forms

THE kinds of connections and variations that can exist between a group of shapes, colors, and textures seem limitless. There are vast families of forms in which all the members have a kind of "family resemblance." In nature we recognize the form of sea shells or of leaves. In visual art a family may be created when a single technique or medium is used. For example, the shapes in the woven poncho in **Fig. A** are all generated, at least in part, by the vertical and horizontal weaving of the loom, which gives them a certain likeness to one another. A Cézanne painting may be made with a single kind of squarish brushstroke, which gives a family

resemblance to sky, trees, and rocks even though they are all different shapes and colors. **(Fig. B).**

Even forms that seem different from one another become part of a visual family when they are part of the same design, print, or painting. This is so because a visual work is a self-contained unit, with its own visual connections and comparisons. The relationships between the shapes, colors, and textures all take place within the boundaries of the frame or the edges of the page, the *visual field*.

In this sense, a piece of visual art works like what scientists call a *closed system*. In a closed

A

system, physical forces are bottled up and sealed off from the surrounding environment. The forces in a closed system cannot disappear; they can only change their form and appear somewhere else in the system. If air is blown into one end of a plumbing system, for example, the air pressure changes to water pressure and then the water pressure at the other end goes up.

Similarly, when something is done in one area of a design, something else must be done in another area. Every mark, ideally, will have repercussions throughout the design. To recognize this phenomenon is to work relationally in the visual arts.

It is this kind of relatedness that can make families out of even the most diverse shapes and colors. The association may be a forced one, of course, created by the confines of the frame, but it is no less powerful.

Also see: Flatness: Grouping, p. 60
Flatness: Mark Making, p. 62

Figure A. Ica poncho. Peruvian. Pre-Columbian. (The Metropolitan Museum of Art; The Michael C. Rockefeller Memorial Collection; Bequest of Nelson A. Rockefeller, 1979)
Figure B. Paul Cézanne, "Mont-Sainte-Victoire." 1904–1906. (Philadelphia Museum of Art; George W. Elkins Collection)

B

Gestalt

O NE of the most persuasive and coherent ways of looking at visual forces has developed from the writings of a group of psychologists who were influenced by certain scientific researchers in Germany and the United States in the early part of this century.

These scientists were interested in finding out how we perceive things, that is, how we take in information through our senses, and organize that information with our minds. Their theories, a result of their observations and experiments, formed the basis of the *Gestalt* school of psychology. *Gestalt* is a more or less untranslatable word, usually rendered in English as "shape" or "form" but also encompassing the notion of configuration, pattern, structure, and wholeness. The basic premise of the Gestaltists is that a visual event is something different from the sum of its parts. The pieces interact and the interaction changes them. When we look at a face, we see not only two eyes, a nose, a mouth, but a configuration, a *gestalt*; the pieces are put together in a certain order, and it is this ordering of the parts that we recognize even more than the parts themselves **(Fig. A).** Thus when artists put things together, they always get something new, something different from a catalogue of the shapes and colors used.

We perceive visual events, then, as wholes which we grasp at once. We do not see by a process of compiling bits of information, but we see large patterns of forces which we recognize as unified.

What the Gestaltists demonstrated that is relevant to visual studies is that the eye is an outpost of the brain, and that the information the eye collects is organized in certain ways by the brain whether we wish it to be or not. Visual perception, the partnership of eye and brain, is not simply a system of passive receivers, a blank slate continually being written on with new messages. Perception is intelligent and often will organize sights, sounds, and events that objectively are not organized. For example, try tap-

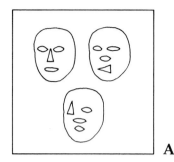

A

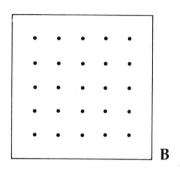

B

ping out a steady rhythm of single beats on the nearest tabletop. After a moment or two you will start to hear the beats in groups. Objectively, you are tapping one-one-one-one, but what you hear will be one-two-one-two-one-two or one-two-three-one-two-three. Or look at the regular patterns of dots in **Fig. B.** You will see, instead of regularity, changing patterns of squares and bars crisscrossing the field.

Many visual phenomena such as grouping, closure, and simplicity demonstrate Gestalt principles. This doesn't mean that this way of perceiving was invented by scientists. Artists have been seeing intelligently for thousands of years before the word *Gestalt* was coined. Since this book is about the conscious organization of visual forms, however, it is helpful for us to understand in more conscious ways things that artists have always intuited.

In this book we will be examining visual relationships and visual forces. We will look at the ways in which shapes and compositions move; how forms bend, push, and rise; how areas expand and contract; how shapes, colors, and other visual elements affect one another. None of these things actually happen in a printed, painted, or drawn design, of course, but the *language* of physical forces can help us to describe what we see in a two-dimensional image. Seeing means experiencing qualities like gravity, pressure, tension, and balance through our eyes.

Seeing, to us as artists, means being conscious of those things that anyone can see but that most people fail to notice.

Also see: Clarity & Ambiguity, p. 26
Grouping, p. 60
How Are Shapes Generated? p. 120
Simple Shape/Complex Shape, p. 122
Gradients (Space, Tonal Gradients, Gradients, and Movement), pp. 74, 178, 158

Rose Window, Church of S. Agostino, Palermo, c. 1300.

Unity
and
Variety

2

Introduction

IN addition to physical needs such as food, clothing, and shelter, human beings have psychological or emotional needs. One of these is the need to establish a balance between sameness and variety in the things we experience. Long days of repeating the same task are dull, but equally unpleasant can be the alternative of a patternless, chaotic existence. We need in our lives both expectability and surprise, order and variety.

Good visual art satisfies our intuitive need for experiences that contain elements both of variety and of repetition and order. These elements need not be in a fifty/fifty mixture. A work of art may push the principle of *unity* to an extreme, as in the Brancusi sculpture in **Fig. A,** which is made of only one, extremely refined, part, or it may opt instead for the richness offered by *variety,* as in the head by Rodin in **Fig. B.** In both cases, we sense something of unity along with some sense of variety.

Figure A. Constantin Brancusi, ''Sculpture for the Blind.'' c. 1916. (Philadelphia Museum of Art; Louise and Walter Arensberg Collection)

Figure B. Auguste Rodin, ''Mask of the Man with a Broken Nose.'' 1864. Bronze. (Hirshhorn Museum and Sculpture Garden, Smithsonian Institution; Gift of Joseph H. Hirshhorn, 1966)

A

UNITY AND VARIETY

Order

"Order is the degree and kind of lawfulness governing the relations among parts of an entity." (RUDOLPH ARNHEIM)

A strict order or set of laws governs where windows, doors, sculptures, and other decorations go in the façade of a Gothic cathedral (**Fig. A**). Not only is the cathedral highly orderly, but there is a very specific kind of order ruling its design. It is organized in a hierarchy. Just as the society of the Middle Ages was a social pyramid with many serfs at the bottom and a few nobles and churchmen at the top, the pieces of the cathedral façade all fit into predetermined levels or niches.

The kind of order involved in **Fig. B**, a Chinese ornamental garden, is less strict. Masses of plants, different kinds of trees, and irregular rock formations are put into precise places but then are left to grow, to change with the seasons or the shifting light and weather. It is a more casual looking kind of order, and it has more than one focal point. It can be seen as a series of different systems of order, with rocks, trees, and architecture arranged to complement one another.

What these two kinds of order have in common is that they both arrange different elements—shapes, colors, and textures—to play dominant or subordinate roles, like actors in a play. In the cathedral, the great entranceway is the star of the ensemble, occupying the center of the large horizontal band that marks the street level of the building. The rose window is almost as important visually, since it is framed by the entire façade. Imagine that a subordinate element, such as the left-hand tower, is moved to the center of the façade. In this position it would become the main element, even if it were flanked by two rose windows.

The ingredients of the Chinese garden work more like a company of actors whose roles are constantly shifting. From one angle, a house or pavilion may be visually dominant. From another position in the garden, a viewer may see a beautiful grouping of trees and stone as a centerpiece, with the architecture serving as a backdrop.

Both these kinds of order are fairly complex. In the cathedral, systems and subsystems are created to deal with the many different shapes, sizes, and textures. In the garden a constellation of more or less equal and complementary systems is created, each of which contains its own hierarchy, as a large rock mass may contain smaller subshapes.

In our sense of the word, disorder does not exist. There are only *levels* of order, either more or less complex webs of relationship and connection. The cathedral has many interlocking tiers of order. A child's room, covered with an even scattering of toys, books, and clothes, also has relationships, but they are one-on-one. Every object, whatever its size, shape, or color, has the same visual importance as every other object. The scattering creates a visual equality of position and subsumes everything into a single system. No subsystems or large groupings can be formed. Rather than the viewer's seeing differences, everything becomes the same, in a sense.

It is worth noting that, as artists, we can *find* order—in the tangled growth of a forest, in the structure of the human figure, in the apparent chaos of a child's room—and we can also *create* order, out of the materials at hand—form, shape, and color. Most works of art do a little of both.

When an artist is faced with communicating a theme as orderly as the social levels of medieval society, the subject can be conveyed by a visual hierarchy. Seurat, however, in "La Grande Jatte" (**Fig. C**) deals with a different view of social levels. His late nineteenth-century city people are part of a society whose strict social divisions are beginning to come apart; the older, orderly pyramid of an agricultural society is being replaced by a population with no particular social ties to one another, new arrivals to Paris from many villages and suburbs. The theme is the breakdown of a society from a complex order (like the cathedral) to a simple order

---

Figure A. Cathedral of Notre Dame, Paris. 1163–1250. (Courtesy of TWA—Trans World Airline)

A

(like the child's room). Figures are scattered rather than formed into ranks, but the design is still highly organized. Seurat stresses the spaces between figures as emblems of emotional and social apartness, and he uses a system of modular proportions (the space between two figures, for example, is twice the length of another figure). Even without explanation and analysis, it is easy to see that the painting could not have been done blindfolded. The sense of disorder that is one theme of the picture is conveyed by an orderly arrangement.

The graphic image in **Fig. D** conveys another kind of disorder: the "out-of-order" sense of a bad emotional relationship and its possible effect on health. Could the image have been made (even partly) by throwing the shapes over one's shoulder without looking? In visual art the sense of disorder is often a theme, but it is always conveyed by organization and choice, that is, by order.

Also see: Hierarchy & Subdivision, p. 28

Proportional Systems, p. 38

Figure B. Chinese ornamental garden.

Figure C. Georges Seurat, "Sunday Afternoon on the Island of La Grande Jatte." 1884–1886. (Courtesy of the Art Institute of Chicago; Helen Birch Bartlett Memorial Collection)

Figure D. Gottschalk & Ash Ltd., Brochure Cover. (Courtesy of Hoffman-LaRoche Ltd.)

B

C

The roots
of marital tension

D Patterns of Tension No. 6

Harmony/Dissonance

A

A design or a composition is a whole visual experience in that it has a general character, which may be gay or severe, rigid or flowing, tense or relaxed. This overall quality results from the fitting together of bits and pieces, each with its own quality of shape, light, or color.

Often when we talk about visual forces, we use a term found in music—*harmony*. When we play the notes C, E, and G at the same time on a piano, they form a harmonious sound called a chord. The chord is like a "fourth sound" different from the three notes that comprise it. This chord has a feeling of satisfying completeness. The notes seem to "go well together" to form a musical sound-structure. If we play C, E, and F instead of G, the combination seems incomplete. A sense of restful completeness is replaced by an unfinished, restless feeling. Our ear seems to have a built-in preference for one kind of sound combination over another.

Similarly, in visual art there are shapes, colors, and sizes which, when put together, seem to form configurations or units that appear stable and complete. *Harmony* in visual art refers to this feeling of restful completeness. We can find this visual calm in Poussin's "Holy Family on the Steps" **(Fig. A)**. The solidly seated triangular group of figures, the horizontal platform that supports them, and the vertical accents that bracket them echo and contribute to the restrained but alive feeling, the composition completed and contained, which is the theme of the work.

In contrast, an image of dissonance is conveyed in Picasso's "Demoiselles d'Avignon" **(Fig. B)** by a fragmenting of the form, the breakup of larger movements into smaller ones, and a stylistic fracturing as well. A strongly dissonant element is Picasso's use of the different and conflicting styles that operate within the work. The simple broad forms of the heads on the left are very different from the more complex, masklike heads on the right. Color changes are abrupt and violent, sometimes cutting across the figures without regard for the anatomy. At the same time, this destruction of conventional form results in another kind of unity by creating a web of triangular shapes throughout. Parts of

B

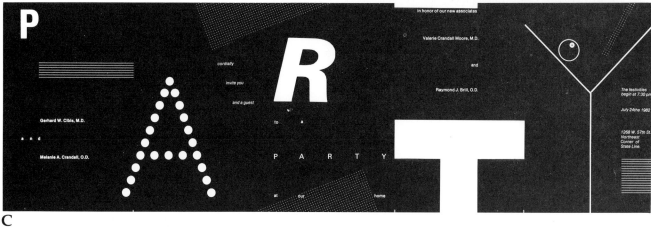

C

Figure A. Nicholas Poussin, ''Holy Family on the Steps.'' 1648. (National Gallery of Art, Washington; Samuel H. Kress Collection, 1952)

Figure B. Pablo Picasso, ''Les Demoiselles d'Avignon.'' 1907. (Collection, The Museum of Modern Art, New York; Acquired through the Lillie P. Bliss Bequest)

Figure C. Lonn Beaudry, ''Invitation: Party.''

the anatomy, drapery folds, even the fruit-laden table in the foreground, are shattered into small triangular vectors.

These examples represent extremes of harmony and dissonance in a design. The type layout in **Fig. C,** a party invitation, juxtaposes different type weights and styles to emphasize dissonance, the noisy and unstructured atmosphere of an informal party. But the design must also be harmonious enough to legibly convey information about the time and place, and the vertical/horizontal alignment of the text creates the needed clarity. Because only a small amount of information needs to be conveyed, the viewer can handle size changes and shifts of position that would be unbearably chaotic and illegible in a longer, more densely packed text.

Also see: Grouping, p. 60
Tension & Shape, p. 132
Color: Harmony & Dissonance, p. 204

Balance

Most people, asked to come up with a simple visual image of balance, would likely imagine two dishes on a scale, each holding equal weight, or perhaps two equally powerful teams engaged in a tug of war, a rope stretched taut between them. In both instances the picture that comes to mind is still and symmetrical. However, just as a small piece of lead will equal a huge pile of feathers on a scale, or two adults equal the strength of a dozen children pulling on a rope, balance can, in a subtle and complex way, be built out of inequalities.

Visual balance takes into account many factors. Size, color, value, shape, orientation, and location all affect our sense of the visual "weight" of a form. Unless a design is absolutely symmetrical, we are always balancing unequal forces in it.

What, then, do we mean by visual balance? We mean the final, overall resolution of opposing forms and forces, the establishment of a "gestalt" that on the one hand seems complete and ordered, but that also clearly includes the lively opposition of forms, shapes, and colors. Visual balance can look as elegant, reduced, and refined as the photograph in **Fig. A,** or as visually and psychologically complex as the painting in **Fig. B,** in which figures, shapes, directions, colors, and spaces relate in a scheme as fragile and breathtaking as a highwire act.

Balance is always dynamic and lively. What is being balanced is not dead weight, but visual forces, movements and countermovements, combinations of unequal qualities which compensate for one another in the larger visual pattern. The painting by Richard Diebenkorn in **Fig. C** is a good example of this complex kind of balance. A big shape is answered by a small one, a color on top is compared with a color near the bottom, a light is balanced against a dark, a horizontal against a vertical. All of these forces are the product of a decision-making process which may be thought out in advance or may take place right on the tip of the brush. Even though intuition and accident may play a role, the process is still decisive.

Also see: Gestalt, p. 6
Weight of Shape, p. 130
Weight of Value, p. 174
Weight of Color, p. 212

Figure A. Eugène Atget, "Magasin, avenue des Gobelins." 1925. (Collection, The Museum of Modern Art, New York; The Abbott-Levy Collection; Partial gift of Shirley C. Burden)

Figure B. Peter Paul Rubens, "The Meeting of Abraham and Melchizedek." c. 1625. (National Gallery of Art, Washington; Gift of Syma Busiel, 1958)

Figure C. Richard Diebenkorn, "Man and Woman in a Large Room." 1957. (Hirshhorn Museum and Sculpture Garden, Smithsonian Institution; Gift of Joseph H. Hirshhorn Foundation, 1966)

A

B

C

Tension

WHEN we look at any visual structure, we see visual forces, which we describe in physical terms. We perceive that shapes or compositions in a painting push and pull and twist, even though there is no real pushing or pulling among the forms of a design. This sense of push and pull, of opposition and resolution, is the life pulse of any work. When we increase the feeling of such visual forces at work, make them seem more powerful or emphatic, we increase *visual tension.*

Visual tension can be expressed in a number of ways, all involving some degree of distortion, deformation, or resistance. Some examples will help to clarify this idea.

In Lyubov Popova's "Architectonic Painting" **(Fig. A),** a light, four-sided shape is visually tense because it appears to be a deformed square, stretched and pulled in different directions. Visual force is added to the balanced, symmetrical forces that help a square to sit solidly. The same kind of distortion makes an egg seem to be a tense and lively form when compared with a sphere **(Fig. B).**

In Alexei Gan's typography **(Fig. C)** the exaggerated vertical thrust of the typeface is a deformation of the letterforms that are usually more compact and earthbound. Notice that along with the almost elastic sense of vertical "stretch," there is a sense of sideways compression and squeezing. This tension answers the vertical tension of the design. The sense of compression also affects the spaces in between the type; the intervals between the capital letters and blocks of type are narrowly pushed together. Throughout the design, we perceive shapes and spaces being pushed and pulled out of their "normal" proportions or positions.

Visual tension can also be created by the placement of forms in a composition. Certain areas in a visual field, such as the center or the edge, have a visual magnetism which seems to attract shapes. When a shape or a line is placed *near* such an area, the pull between the shape and the position it seems to "want to be in" creates a sense that forces are pulling the forms from their normal position. Shapes within a composition can exert similar forces upon one

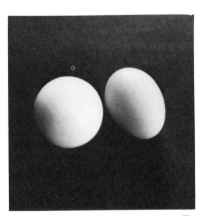

B

A

another, attracting and repelling each other as intervals between them narrow, and creating tension.

The lithograph by Pierre Bonnard in **Fig. D** is made of shapes placed off center and close to the edge. The line of coaches solidly stuck to the upper edge of the field and the stable, bell-like forms of the caped women on the upper left are pleasantly opposed by a very different group of shapes, irregular and full of movement, on the lower right.

Also see: The Field, p. 46
The Edge, p. 54
Tension & Shape, p. 132
Directed Tension, p. 156

Figure A. Lyubov Popova, ''Architectonic Painting.'' 1917. (Collection, The Museum of Modern Art, New York; Philip Johnson Fund)

Figure C. Alexei Gan, ''First Exhibition/Contemporary Architects/S.A.'' 1928. (Collection, The Museum of Modern Art, New York; Gift of Alfred H. Barr, Jr.)

Figure D. Pierre Bonnard, ''Screen.'' 1897. (Collection, The Museum of Modern Art, New York; Abby Aldrich Rockefeller Fund)

C

D

Symmetry

SYMMETRY occurs when the visual elements on one side of a configuration are mirrored exactly on the opposite side. When this mirroring happens entirely around a central point, it is called *radial symmetry*, as might be seen in the round window of a Romanesque cathedral **(Fig. A)**. When the right side echoes the left or the top echoes the bottom, we have *bilateral symmetry*, the kind that we see in a Rorschach test **(Fig. B)** or along the bank of a still pond. Symmetry is a powerful and rather rigid way of organizing a design. In such a composition it is easy to see the sense of unity, a centralized "master plan" controlling the smaller parts. The symmetry of the African relief plaque in **Fig. C** creates an image of royal formality, of figures which do not interact with natural forces in the same way you and I do. The potential liveliness of the forms themselves is held in tense check by the near symmetrical mirror image of right and left.

Symmetry in a design is an obvious way of creating a sense of balance and stillness, as in a pair of scales balancing two equal weights. If symmetry is applied in situations where we normally expect movement, the static or frozen look that it creates may be equally striking. The symmetry of the faces in Edvard Munch's print in **Fig. D,** for example, is eerily motionless, with a staring quality that turns a crowd of strolling people into a gallery of ghosts.

The same frozen quality is an important part of the somewhat dark humor in Tadanori Yokoo's poster in **Fig. E.** The mechanical efficiency with which the composition is arranged is a source of visual comedy, as in a Charlie Chaplin film. The poster satirizes the prissy and overly rational quality of some modern design.

Also see: Left & Right, p. 50
Directed Tension, p. 156

Figure A. Rose Window, Church of S. Agostino, Palermo, c. 1300.

Figure C. Plaque, Court of Benin, Nigeria. 19th–20th century. (The Metropolitan Museum of Art; The Michael C. Rockefeller Memorial Collection; Gift of Nelson A. Rockefeller, 1978)

Figure D. Edvard Munch, "Anxiety." 1896. (Collection, The Museum of Modern Art, New York; Abby Aldrich Rockefeller Fund)

Figure E. Tadanori Yokoo, "Made in Japan, Tadanori Yokoo Having Reached a Climax at the Age of 29, I Was Dead." 1965. (Collection, The Museum of Modern Art, New York; Gift of the Artist)

A

B

C

D

E

Asymmetry

WHEN a composition is arranged asymmetrically, we become aware of the individual identities of shapes and colors. Differences between the various areas are stressed, so variety is more visible than is unity. Although the sense of overall unity may seem less obvious, however, an asymmetrical composition may be every bit as planned as a symmetrical one.

In Piet Mondrian's composition in **Fig. A,** one difference answers another. A small full area, packed with color, counterbalances a larger empty area somewhere else. A square area is contrasted with a rectangular space, and a wide interval coexists with a narrow one. Rather than blending blue into red, or black into white, or vertical into horizontal, each element is conceived as a separate, self-contained unit of color,

shape, and direction. The unity is a bringing together of differences which complement one another like different instruments in an orchestra. The final image is one of order and harmony, but the balance created by the strongly asymmetrical elements is a lively one.

Asymmetry tends to create visual tension, a sense of imbalance and movement, or of a delicate balance carefully achieved, quite different from the stability and stillness of symmetrical organization.

Sassetta used an asymmetrical composition to move the viewer's eye from one episode to another in **Fig. B.** Instead of stillness and gravity, this composition refuses to hold still, tottering back and forth along zig-zag diagonals. The eye glides smoothly from a high point on the left to a low point on the right. Individual figures

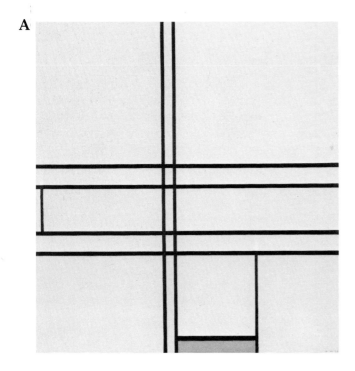

A

B

and small groups form subcompositions, smaller vignettes of action and event within the big picture.

Since asymmetry is a less rigid or centralized method of organization, it is often used to create an informal or casual look. The page in **Fig. C** has the "unarranged" look of objects scattered on a tabletop. The composition was certainly carefully planned to achieve a delicate balance, but the playful sense appropriate to a children's book is preserved.

Also see: Balance, p. 18

Directed Tension, p. 156

Figure A. Piet Mondrian, "Composition with Blue and Yellow." 1935. (Hirshhorn Museum and Sculpture Garden, Smithsonian Institution; Gift of Joseph H. Hirshhorn Foundation, 1972)

Figure B. Sassetta, "The Meeting of St. Anthony and St. Paul." c. 1440. (National Gallery of Art, Washington; Samuel H. Kress Collection)

Figure C. Leo Lionni, from "Let's Make Rabbits." 1982. (Copyright © 1982 by Leo Lionni. Reprinted by permission of Pantheon Books, a Division of Random House, Inc.)

C

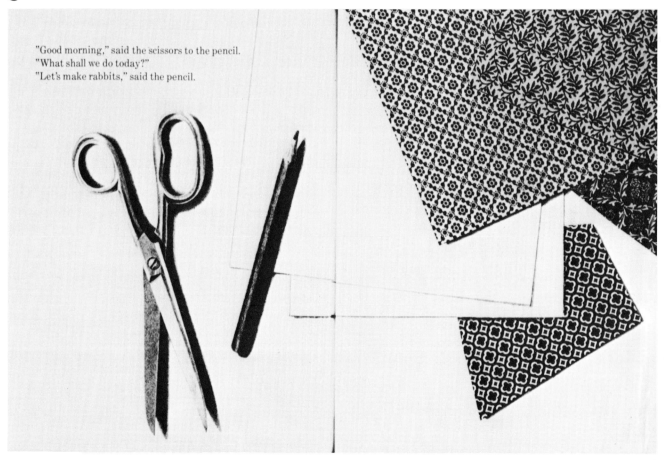

"Good morning," said the scissors to the pencil.
"What shall we do today?"
"Let's make rabbits," said the pencil.

Clarity & Ambiguity

THE eye seeks clarity in a visual pattern, that is, the eye must be able to tell what a design is trying to say. Is the shape in **Fig. A** supposed to be a square or an irregularly shaped trapezoid? Is the circle in **Fig. B** meant to be on center or off center? Are the two shapes in **Fig. C** supposed to be different or were they simply ineptly made by an untrained hand trying for two identical shapes?

Each of these visual patterns is unclear, seeming to waver between two possibilities. When that happens, the forms seem to be out of place and wanting to move. We feel some correcting hand is needed either to push **Fig. A** into a square or to lengthen two of its sides, and to move the circle in **Fig. B** either into or further from the center.

This straining kind of visual movement is different from the clearly directed tensions found in a dynamic composition. It is a visual *ambiguity*, which our visual mechanism tries to resolve through processes called *leveling* and *sharpening*. If any of the patterns in Figs. A, B, or C were flashed for an instant onto a screen, we would probably remember them as unambiguous—either as perfected, as in **Fig. D,** or as clearly distorted, as in **Fig. E.** The eye/brain has

a built-in propensity for order which will make us see things clearly even when they are not clear.

Order is achieved when the pushes and pulls in a composition can be clearly understood by the eye, when we have no doubt about the direction in which a form is moving or being pulled, or about the nature of its relationship to an ideal shape or position. Movement or distortion need not be dramatic, but it must be sufficiently unambiguous to be perceived as intentional.

Some kinds of ambiguity can be desirable. Multiple or alternative readings, like metaphors in speech, can add levels of meaning and enrich the image. In the painting by Georges Braque **(Fig. F),** we can see both the full face and the profile of the model, two distinct and unambiguous images which seem simultaneously to occupy the same space. It is important to note that each of the readings is unambiguous in the sense that we have been using the term. We are not confused about which reading is intended. We are quite sure that we are meant to see both.

The extreme clarity of geometrically based design, its legibility, sense of organization, and careful placement, have made it an immensely

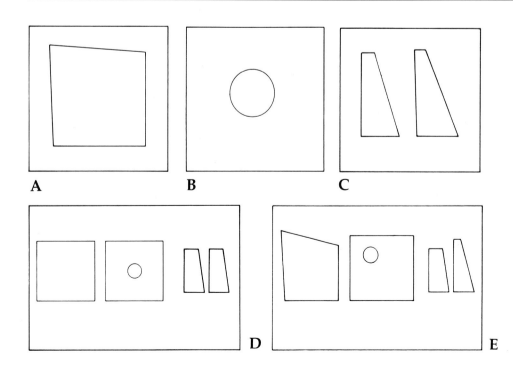

A

B

C

D

E

tempting direction for artists in this century. The fact that there are systems such as grids, a basic set of rules and tools for making geometric form, as well as the widely held feeling that geometry reflects our own highly mechanized society, also have not hurt its popularity. In addition, the growing interest in computers as design tools has also resulted in graphics that have a hard-edged look, at times inappropriately boxy and brittle, more like diagrams than anything else.

The recognition now that extreme clarity does not necessarily make for art, or is even all that interesting, has led to a questioning of hard design and to another thoughtful look by artists at the qualities of soft design, organic or irregular shape, the sense of hand-making, intuition, and the lively surprises that sometimes result. If the shape we want to make is a circle, we automatically follow the rules for construction of a circle, a predetermined shape. To design an irregular shape, however, we must make personal choices about degrees of clarity and complexity, about angle and direction. The forms in **Fig. G** are the result of this kind of approach.

Since each attitude toward design has its own uses and limitations, and since hard and softer approaches are both ancient ways of thinking about form, both are worth a careful look. Yet a certain amount of intuition is always necessary, even in computer graphics, just as a sense of structure and order is a major component in the organization of any kind of handwork.

Also see: Geometric/Organic Shape, p. 126
Visual Information, p. 236

Figure F. Georges Braque, ''Woman Painting.'' 1936. (Courtesy, Collection of Consolidated Foods Corporation)
Figure G. Henri Matisse, ''Beasts of the Sea.'' Dated (19)50. (National Gallery of Art, Washington; Ailsa Mellon Bruce Fund, 1973)

F

G

Hierarchy & Subdivision

A

IN most works of art we are faced with putting together differences: a large shape and a small one, a yellow against a blue, a line and a soft smudge of tone. Although every piece of a composition may be necessary, our eyes establish scales of importance, from primary visual elements to secondary to tertiary. Organizing things by grouping them into divisions and subdivisions is a basic requirement for unifying any configuration containing unequal visual elements. A visual hierarchy allows us to see the whole structure, the large organization that determines where every part fits, while also permitting us to see each individual part as an isolated unit with a place in the whole.

Hierarchical organization occurs throughout nature. For example, a tree can be broken down into a main unit (the trunk), which supports subdivisions (the large boughs), which support smaller branches, which carry twigs and leaves. We may not necessarily move our eyes from larger limbs to smaller limbs. We can look anywhere we like on a tree. Still, we see that an order of large to small is present regardless of how we look at it.

A typical hierarchical composition in painting is the "Alba Madonna" of Raphael **(Fig. A).** Here a triangular mass is created by the figures. The area of greatest prominence, the peak of the triangle, is occupied by the head of the Madonna. As we move down the left hand slope of the triangle, we come to the Christ child, a secondary element in this group, and then to the infant St. John, the subordinate character.

The hierarchy in the Raphael is almost as obvious as it is in the tree. A less centralized composition, like the poster in **Fig. B,** also has its divisions and subdivisions. There is a scale of weights, from the heavy "Yale" to the less heavy "Norfolk" and so on down to the small text, and this large to small movement of the forms also shows us the order in which the visual information is to be read.

Still another kind of hierarchy is estab-

B

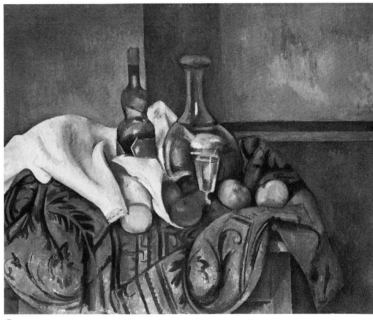

C

lished in Paul Cézanne's painting in **Fig. C.** The most important visual division is the one between foreground, a table loaded with a clutter of objects, and background, a subdivided wall. The foreground then subdivides into drapery, fruit, and bottles, and each of these subdivisions contains its own smaller units of direction and color. The drapery can be broken down into lighter and darker material. The bottles can be subdivided into body and neck, and these areas too contain smaller color zones, each of which contains still smaller shapes, colors, and textures.

As in any hierarchy, this seemingly natural organization helps us to see the whole in the right order. We do not read through a two-dimensional image in the same linear way that you are now reading through this page—first one word, then the next, in order, until a complete idea or sentence is formed. To read in this way

Figure A. Raphael, ''The Alba Madonna.'' c. 1510. (National Gallery of Art, Washington; Andrew W. Mellon Collection)

Figure B. Robert Jensen, ''Yale at Norfolk.'' (Courtesy of the Designer)

Figure C. Paul Cézanne, ''Still Life with Peppermint Bottle.'' c. 1894. (National Gallery of Art, Washington; Chester Dale Collection, 1962)

Also see: Grids, p. 40
Figure/Ground, p. 70
Microstructure/Macrostructure, p. 110

means that we move through time, rather like a burning fuse. A photograph or a painting does not reveal its forms in this way. Rather, its hierarchies and subdivisions allow us to see the whole all at once, simultaneously, and at the same time the parts, separately and in order.

Repetition & Variation

REPETITION, which is related to time and rhythm, is one of the most effective ways to create unity in a composition. It can seem to diminish the individuality or uniqueness of a form. Handled in a mechanical way, repetition may quickly become boring; some sense of variation is a real human need. In **Fig. A** by Andy Warhol the deadening sameness of the image is countered by small variables—changes in light or darkness from one pair of lips to another, slight shifts in position—all signs of life that the eye fastens upon.

Repetition can be used for its cumulative effect, the impact of a single form multiplied, as in the poster in **Fig. B.** Repetition here is like the echo of a great shout, peaking and dying away as the eye moves from left to right.

In Toulouse-Lautrec's lithograph in **Fig. C** the repeated diagonal of three legs is a visual metaphor for the beat of the music. The not-so-subtle rhythm of the can-can is spelled out for the eyes, and Lautrec makes a wry comment about the coordination of the dancers in the angle of the left-hand dancer's leg.

Also see: Mark Making, p. 62
Time, p. 164
Grids, p. 40

Figure A. Andy Warhol, ''Marilyn Monroe's Lips,'' 1962. (Hirshhorn Museum and Sculpture Garden, Smithsonian Institution; Gift of Joseph H. Hirshhorn, 1972)

Figure B. G. Klutsis, ''Fulfilled Plan Great Work.'' 1930. (Collection, The Museum of Modern Art, New York; Purchase Fund)

Figure C. Henri de Toulouse-Lautrec, ''Troup of Mlle. Églantine.'' 1896. (Collection, The Museum of Modern Art, New York; Gift of Abby Aldrich Rockefeller)

A

B

C

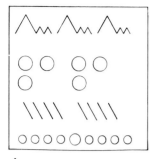

A

B

C

Figure B. Pont du Gard. Near Nîmes, France. Roman, 1st century B.C.

Figure C. Christopher Ozubko and Robert Meganck, ''Double Bill Jazz Concert.'' (Meganck Ozubko Design, Seattle)

Figure D. ''Virgin and Child.'' School of Auvergne, France. c. 1150–1200. (Metropolitan Museum of Art; Gift of J. Pierpont Morgan, 1916)

Figure E. Lester Johnson, ''City Street Scene #7.'' 1978–1979.

D

Rhythm

RHYTHM in music is a way of giving form and shape to time by organizing and subdividing it: 3/4 time has one kind of form, 4/4 time has another. We might "draw" these as the diagrams in **Fig. A.** When the beats in a musical piece become irregular, time becomes unstructured. Obviously, rhythm also means repetition, repetition of the beat and of the interval, or the length of the silence between beats. When there is sufficient repetition, even a slight deviation from the pattern becomes easily noticeable **(Fig. A).**

Visual rhythms are also based on repetition of shapes, colors, or intervals, but there is a greater possibility for flexibility and variety. Whereas music happens primarily in time, with sounds and silences following each other, visual art—even when it is two-dimensional—happens in space, where many things can interact at the same time. Thus subtle and complex kinds of visual rhythm are possible. A design may have a linear rhythm that goes up and down or in and out, a smooth or angular rhythm, the staccato rhythm of a machine gun, or the graceful back and forth of a waltz. A rhythm may be precise and mechanical or irregular and organic.

Simple repetition fuels the stately and rhythmic progress through the landscape of a Roman aqueduct **(Fig. B).** The elegance of its proportions and the reassuring expectability of each arch have the same hypnotic regularity as the sound of the ocean washing onto the beach. The whole is unified by the sameness of shape and interval but is saved from dullness by the visual changes the forms undergo as they march into the distance, becoming smaller to the eye, lighter in color, the smooth curves becoming tenser, adding a necessary secondary element of variety.

In **Fig. C** the broken phrasing of jazz is made visual in a subtle way. The diagonal is repeated at the same angle but at varied intervals from left to right. The weight of the diagonal is varied too, from the most ghostly line of white type to a heavier white bar. Against this constant but changing beat the large letters create a series of irregular angular gestures, ending with the large Z which repeats the angle of the small type.

A more regular rhythm is created by the drapery of the twelfth-century sculpture in **Fig. D.** The curved folds are repeated at equal intervals, gradually expanding in a fluid, wavelike pulse across the form. The beat is repetitive but the form of the arc is flexible.

In the painting by Lester Johnson **(Fig. E)** the figures fit themselves into a slightly mechanical ballet, the repetitive parallels of legs and arms like pistons, creating visual energy across the rectangle as they move up and down, in and out, back and forth.

Also see: Repetition & Variation, p. 30
Stroboscopic Motion, p. 162

E

Arabesque

Arabesque is a word originally used to describe a complicated, interweaving linear composition often found in Arabic art. A similar sinuous, enclosed line can be found in the art of many other periods and cultures.

A beautiful example is the carved box in **Fig. A.** As graceful as any brush drawing, it employs a line that functions as an element with a fluctuating life of its own, whether it is used to draw animals or simply serves as decoration to fill the long horizontal bands at top and bottom.

One of the features of this kind of composition is that it feels contained. The line may wander and waver, but it curves back in upon itself rather than breaking through the framing rectangle. The line itself is not well suited to describing objects in a realistic way, but its abstract quality, its inherent visual interest, appealed to

A

B

C

artists who worked by symbolizing rather than by accurately depicting. This kind of organization is also an attractive alternative to the right-angled quality that often results from use of grids.

Art Nouveau in the early twentieth century is probably the best known movement that made use of the curvilinear arabesque, although the artists were influenced as much by the flowing lines of Japanese woodcut compositions **(Fig. B)** as by Arabic art. Hector Guimard's poster in **Fig. C** is an example of the liveliness of the Art Nouveau arabesque. The letterforms seem to be invaded by visual forces that make them swell, compress, bend, and stretch. The sense of growth and change that we see in the tendrils and leaves of a plant is conveyed by the constantly changing arabesque.

The curved line is also a visual symbol of forces interacting. In the painted relief sculpture by Frank Stella **(Fig. D)** the shapes seem to act on one another. The long curve swooping down from the upper left corner seems to rear back sharply like a wave breaking on a rock, in re-sponse to another curve that blocks its path. The small s-curve in the lower right corner sags under the visual weight of the larger shape above it. Two large question mark shapes appear to rub up against each other and curl away. The design is an ensemble in which forms *do* things to other forms.

Also see: Enclosed Space, p. 94

The Line as Edge: Contour Line, p. 146

Gradients & Movement, p. 158

Figure A. Casket. Southern Italy (probably). 11th or 12th century. (The Metropolitan Museum of Art; Gift of J. Pierpont Morgan, 1917)

Figure B. ''Dancer.'' Attributed to Torii Kiyonobu. (The Metropolitan Museum of Art; Harris Brisbane Dick Fund, 1949)

Figure C. Hector Guimard, ''Exposition Salon du Figaro le Castel Beranger.'' 1900. (Collection, The Museum of Modern Art, New York; Gift of Lillian Nassau)

Figure D. Frank Stella, ''Shoubeegi.'' 1978. (Private Collection)

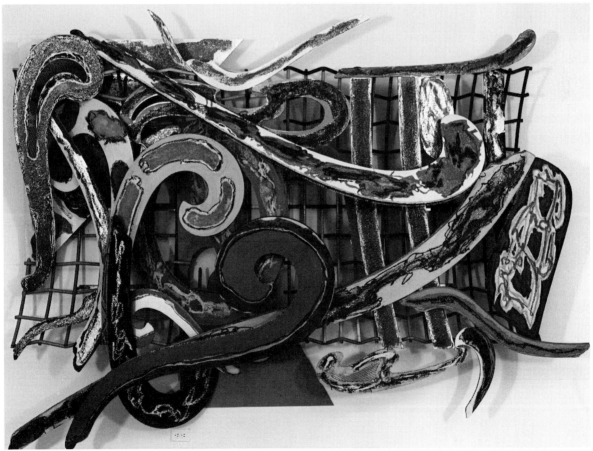

D

Straightness

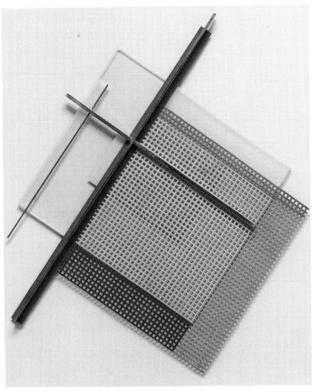

A

HE curved line of the arabesque seems to be constantly acted upon by visual forces that push and pull on it. In contrast, straightness is a visual symbol of noninteraction, a line that doesn't change but rather ignores the forces around it.

In César Domela's wall relief in **Fig. A**, straight lines pass through one another without any sign of interaction. Neither slowed down nor deflected from its course, each line is an independent element, visually isolated from the rest even though it contributes to the overall ensemble of colored areas.

The isolating quality of straightness can be a useful tool when the artist's aim is to highlight individual parts that make up a composition. Straightness gives visual autonomy to the elements of Gerrit Rietveld's chair in **Fig. B.** The chair is broken down into separate planes, and

B

the sense of individual lines in space as the raw material of the designer is made concrete.

Straightness and noninteraction are given a different meaning in Edvard Munch's ''Self-Portrait'' **(Fig. C).** Here the rigidity of the forms creates a sense of emotional isolation. Straitjacketed by the furniture and the verticals of the walls, the room is pervaded with a tense and frozen stillness. The feeling that time has stopped is emphasized by the clock, which echoes the figure of the artist.

Also see: The Impersonal Line, p. 140
Vertical/Horizontal/Diagonal, p. 160

Figure A. César Domela, ''Construction.'' 1929. (Hirshhorn Museum and Sculpture Garden, Smithsonian Institution; Gift of Joseph H. Hirshhorn, 1966)

Figure B. Gerrit Rietveld, ''Red and Blue'' Chair. c. 1918. (Collection, The Museum of Modern Art, New York; Gift of Philip Johnson)

Figure C. Edvard Munch, ''Self-Portrait Between the Clock and the Bed.'' 1940–1942. (Munch Museum, Oslo)

C

Proportional Systems

PROPORTION refers to the relationship between different sizes and shapes in a design, and how these differences fit into the whole structural pattern of the design. A proportional system allows us to create differences and variations in size and shape according to a single, consistent law.

For example, when Alice grows a long neck in Wonderland, we can say that her neck is "out of proportion" when compared with the rest of her body. It seems to be governed by some law of growth *different* from that which governs the rest of her body **(Fig. A)**. A long neck in a painting by Parmigianino **(Fig. B)** is part of a general

A

B

stretching out that operates throughout the whole picture, and so it fits in with the elongated proportions of the rest of the body.

All proportional systems are based on simple numerical ratios that can be strung together, halved, or multiplied to grow complex combinations of form. It is not clear, however, *which* numbers will give us good proportions. The Greeks often used a ratio, sometimes called the Golden Section, in which a small line is to a larger line as the larger line is to the sum of the two. This proportion can be seen in **Fig. C.** Something as simple as a rectangular module or as complicated as the sculpture of a spear carrier in **Fig. D** can be made according to this system. The length of the torso compared with the legs, for example, seems to have been determined according to this proportion. For the Greeks, numbers were the unifying understructure which could be used in carving a nude or figuring out the height/width ratio for a temple.

A different kind of proportional system, based on a square and the rectangle made of two squares, is found in Japanese architecture. The size and shape of the rooms in a classic Japanese house were based on woven floor mats, called Tatami mats **(Fig. E),** whose long side was twice its short side. A single module determined the floor plan and could be multiplied to determine the entire proportion of the room.

Probably the most common proportional system, used in many variations today, can be found in the two-dimensional grid, which is discussed in the next section.

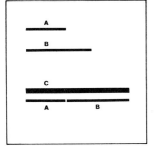

C

Also see: Grids, p. 40

Tension & Shape, p. 132

Figure A. John Tenniel, ''Alice with a Long Neck.'' (from *Alice in Wonderland*)

Figure B. Francesco Parmigianino, ''Madonna with the Long Neck.'' c. 1535. (Uffizi Gallery, Florence)

Figure C. Golden Section proportion.

Figure D. after Polyclitus, ''Spear Carrier.'' c. 450 B.C. (Museo Nazionale, Naples)

Figure E. Tatami mats.

D

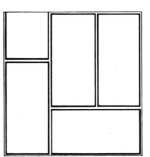

E

Grids

GRIDS are one kind of proportional system, widely used by graphic designers and often found in the work of visual artists in every medium.

A simple grid, shown in **Fig. A,** divides a rectangle into sixteen equal smaller rectangles. Rather than allowing the eye to penetrate into an imaginary three-dimensional space, the lines of the grid shunt the eye up and down and from side to side, keeping us aware of the flat surface of the page.

The grid also encourages us to divide our attention equally over the entire surface. Each rectangle is identical in size and shape to every other rectangle. Each contains the same percentage of area, and there are no important or unimportant areas.

Finally, the smaller subdivisions here all have the same proportions as the large rectangle. Like echoes, they repeat the height/width ratio over and over. The smallest rectangle is a seed out of which the largest one grows. Grids, then, are a means of organizing flat space, creating a scaffolding or skeleton on which to hang and keep track of shapes, lines, and marks. Throughout the design a grid creates a sameness that we can use to organize differences.

Grids need not be as regular as a checkerboard. **Fig. B** shows four very different kinds of grids, and there are an infinite number of variations. Every grid, however, divides the surface in a regular and easily comprehended way, and the location and relationship of every form to every other form in it are clear and logical.

In the drawing in **Fig. C** an implied grid provides the underlying structure on which the flickering brushwork is hung, rather like a trellis supporting the organic growth of a grapevine.

The main characteristic of a grid is its clarity. It provides the means for a clear and simple organization where many different kinds of visual information must be presented with a maximum of legibility. See, for example, the posters in **Fig. D.**

Like any tool, the grid can be used imaginatively or unimaginatively. It can produce a regimented looking, repetitive organization if the artist cannot break out of it when appropri-

ate to do so. Sometimes the authoritative look of a grid inhibits the user and challenges us even more to rely on the judgment of our eyes. The composition by Thomas Eakins in **Fig. E** seems to include the logic of the grid. The shoreline, for instance, divides the painting into two almost equal horizontal bands, and many elements seem to be carefully placed to emphasize vertical and horizontal. However, important forms such as the vertical stake are placed slightly off the grid (and are not quite vertical). We could say that beneath the underlying structure of the grid there is another order—that of intuition.

Also see: Proportional Systems, p. 38

The Field, p. 46

Frontal Recession, p. 88

Figure C. David Smith, ''Untitled II.'' 1961. (Collection of the Whitney Museum of American Art, New York; Gift of Candida Smith)

Figure D. Max Bill, ''Exhibition Posters.'' (1945 and 1951). (Courtesy of the Library of Congress)

Figure E. Thomas Eakins, ''Biglin Brothers Turning the Stake.'' 1873. (The Cleveland Museum of Art; Hinman B. Hurlbut Collection)

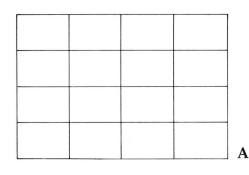

A

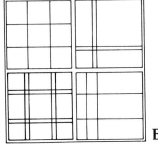

B

C

D

Moderne Kunst

aus der Sammlung Peggy Guggenheim

Kunsthaus Zürich

kunstgewerbemuseum zürich

USA baut

9. september – 7. oktober 1945

E

Felix Vallotton, ''A Street in Paris.'' (The Metropolitan Museum
of Art, New York; Robert Lehman Collection, 1975)

Flatness

3

Introduction

A

THERE is a basic difference between the way we see the world around us and the way we see something on a flat page, and different sets of rules apply to the two kinds of "seeing."

First of all, we see the world in three dimensions: things that appear to be round or to be separated really are. The surface of a canvas or a page, on the other hand, is flat, two-dimensional. Anyone who has ever looked at a "3-D" picture or a hologram knows that a three-dimensional illusion looks very different from a photograph or a painting.

We see the world out of two eyes, which record two separate and slightly different images that are combined by the brain into one

three-dimensional image. Try closing one eye. When we lose binocular (two-eyed) vision, depth becomes muffled and our ability to judge distance is weakened.

The painting by Peter Paul Rubens in **Fig. A** is one artist's witty and knowing comment on flatness. At first glance a typical Baroque painting full of movement and sculptural space, we gradually notice a grand visual joke. The central scene becomes, at the edges, a huge tapestry supported by "real" angels. The folds of the tapestry sweep into and behind the "real" columns and moldings at bottom and on the right, while two figures at bottom right seem to emerge from a stairwell, or do they belong in the tapestry? Rubens deliberately confuses the issues of space and flatness, raising the question "What is real?"

In addition, when we see in the world, our eyes continually jump about from one thing to another. You may look at someone's face, for example, then shift your eye to his hand, then glance over to the corner of the room, then back to your friend's nose, all in very quick succession. As your eye moves along, one thing disappears and another becomes the center of attention. In a two-dimensional image, things do not appear and disappear in this way. All the shapes and colors are presented simultaneously.

Furthermore, our eyes can change focus, so that an object seen clearly in the foreground may become a blur as we look at something further away (and may sharpen up again as we refocus on it). The elements on a page are all frozen, fixed in one form or another.

In ways that we don't always notice, things look different when we place them on a flat surface. When we move from the real world to the page, we *translate* from one visual language (three-dimensionality) into another, which has a grammar and a logic of its own.

Also see: Flatness & Space Together, p. 102

Figure A. Peter Paul Rubens, "The Meeting of Abraham and Melchizedek." c. 1625. (National Gallery of Art, Washington; Gift of Syma Busiel)

The Field

ONE important difference between the world around us and the page is that the shapes, colors, and lines on a two-dimensional surface are framed by the edges of that page or surface. The edges create a *visual field*, of a specific shape, a closed-off arena in which visual elements co-exist, interact, and affect one another.

The environment that surrounds us, by contrast, is a parade of visual events, one thing after another, an unframed and continuous fabric of sights that come and go, extending in all directions as far as the eye can see.

Frequently the shape of the visual field that we work on is straight edged and rectangular. The two horizontal and vertical sides visually "echo" an important fact about the world around us: that the force of gravity pulls us downward, and that we exert our own counter force which enables us to stand or move and resist that downward pull. The rectangular field is solid looking, stable, somewhat static, and clear. It "sits" sturdily on its bottom edge. If we want to, we can repeat the vertical/horizontal movements inside the rectangle in an orderly way and make a grid on which to hang shape and color. For an artist like Piet Mondrian (**Fig. A**) this echoing and balancing of the horizontal and vertical, forces that to him were a visual metaphor for body and spirit, were an intensely expressive activity.

Artists work on fields of other shapes as well. Each of these shapes is a dish on which to serve up color and form, but even as blank frames they are far from empty. The oval or round field is less likely to stay put visually than the square. It "rolls," seems to rotate or expand outward. The center of an oval or circular field is more strongly felt than the middle of a rectangle (**Fig. B**).

The irregularly shaped field is a breeding ground for visual energy. Even empty, it has thrusts, countermovements, bulges, internal forces jostling one another (**Fig. C**). It can be an aggressive shape which will compete for attention with the forms placed within it.

Each format has its own special qualities and therefore its own uses and limitations. The

A

irregular field may be useful for an artist who aims for a sense of movement and expressive fragmentation, while the oval may appeal because of the visual tension created by its expansion in one direction. The rectangular field offers a sense of gravity or heaviness. The important thing to remember is that each visual field is already charged with visual energy before any marks or colors are placed on its surface.

Also see: Tension & Shape, p. 132
Vertical/Horizontal/Diagonal, p. 160
Simple Shape/Complex Shape, p. 122
Grids, p. 40

B

C

Figure A. Piet Mondrian, "Composition 1916." 1916. (Collection, Solomon R. Guggenheim Museum, New York)

Figure B. François Boucher, "Madonna and Child with St. John and Angels." 1765. (The Metropolitan Museum of Art, New York; Gift of Adelaide Milton de Groot in memory of the de Groot and Hawley families, 1966)

Figure C. Elizabeth Murray, "Popeye." 1982. (Collection, The Museum of Modern Art, New York; Gift of Abby Aldrich Rockefeller, by exchange)

Top & Bottom

THE upper and lower parts of a visual field are different. In the world around us, forms are heavier and more numerous near the ground and progressively fewer and lighter as we look up. Our sense of gravity is also involved. When we see things rise, such as an athlete jumping or a ball thrown in the air, we "see" energy and power being released, gravity being overcome. When we see something sink to the ground, we see a relaxation or a surrender to the downward pull.

Similarly, in a visual field the higher shapes on the page or canvas seem more full of visual energy and slightly bigger than the same shape placed lower down. Forms placed near the bottom of the field seem emptier, pulled down by the visual magnetism of the bottom edge **(Fig. A).**

If we look at the circle in the painting by Paul Klee in **Fig. B,** we feel its weight and mass hanging heavily from the top of the image. Turn the book upside down and the same form, now at the bottom, feels relaxed, lighter, at ease, and we begin to notice instead the dark rectangle above it as looming and massive.

Artists can place shapes to achieve a neu-

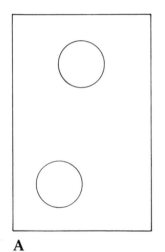

A

B

tral balance, or a visual evenness between top and bottom. For example, suppose you are cutting a rectangular opening in a mat in order to frame a drawing. If all four sides of the mat are equally wide, the opening will seem to be placed too low in the mat. When the bottom edge is made slightly larger·than the others, thus raising the opening in the rectangle, the opening feels comfortably placed **(Fig. C).**

Alvin Coburn's photograph in **Fig. D** balances the form of a cloud against a mountain peak below it. Positioned close to the upper edge, the cloud is ''pulled'' upward by the vi-

sual magnetism that an edge exerts on any nearby form. It also gains visual weight by being placed high in the image. The range of lights and darks plays over it, sculpting it into a massive three-dimensional form in contrast to the flattened silhouettes of the mountains which rest gently on the bottom edge. The combination of visual heaviness and lift make an image of titanic force.

Typographers designing letterforms make them slightly heavier toward the bottom so they do not appear top heavy. Letters that seem to be equal on top and bottom, such as S or E, will often look unbalanced when turned upside down **(Fig. E).**

We do not always want equality between top and bottom. Where legibility and visual clarity are important, the most delicately and precisely balanced arrangement may indeed be best. In other situations, however, an unequal relation between bottom and top may offer the potential for an unstable and tensely expressive visual image.

Also see: Space Cues: Vertical Location, p. 80
Weight of Shape, p. 130
The Edge, p. 54
The Center, p. 52

Figure B. Paul Klee, ''Red Balloon.'' 1922. (Collection, Solomon R. Guggenheim Museum, New York)

Figure D. Alvin Langdon Coburn, Plate 3 from ''The Cloud.'' 1912. (Collection, The Museum of Modern Art, New York; Purchase)

C

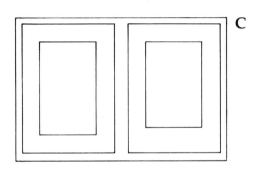

D

E

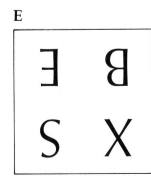

Left & Right

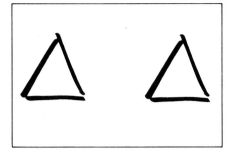

A

B

LIKE the top and bottom of a visual field, the left and right look and feel different to the viewer. If two identical shapes are placed on the left and right sides of a field **(Fig. A),** the right-hand shape will generally seem slightly larger or more powerful. This phenomenon obviously has consequences for the printmaker, for instance, whose work is usually reversed when transferred to paper, or for the book designer, whose single page will become half of a larger composition. All artists consider these factors as lively compositional elements to be thought about as consciously as shape, line or color.

There is also a tendency to scan with our eyes from left to right. It is unclear whether our doing this is due in part to the almost universal practice of reading from left to right, or whether reading from left to right is the result of this left-to-right scan. Hokusai uses this visual tendency effectively to reinforce the subject matter in his print of a landscape buffeted by a gust of wind **(Fig. B).** The composition is weighted on the left, with two trees and the mass of Mount Fuji anchoring it. The rightward movement of the wind is aided by the angle of the trees, the long, downward slope of the mountain, the blowing leaves and paper, and especially the left to right scanning of the viewer. If we look at it in a mirror, however, the forces are dramatically

Figure B. Hokusai, ''A Gust of Wind at Ejiri'' from *The 36 Views of Fuji.* c. 1831–1833. (The Metropolitan Museum of Art, New York; Purchase; Rogers Fund, 1936)

Figure C. Thomas Gainsborough, ''Mr. and Mrs. Andrews.'' c. 1749. (Reproduced by courtesy of the Trustees, The National Gallery, London)

Figure D. Camille Corot, ''Volterra.'' 1834. (Louvre Museum, Paris)

Figure E. Lori Wynn and Dennis Thompson, Letterhead: ''Friends of Recreation and Parks.'' (Dennis Thompson, Jody Thompson, Lori Wynn; The Thompson Design Group, San Francisco)

changed. Instead of ''riding the wind,'' our left to right glance now bumps into or moves against it. Our eyes are forced to climb the long background slope.

A composition that is weighted on the left allows an easier right-hand movement. When we look at Gainsborough's portrait of two landowners and their estate **(Fig. C),** our eyes glide easily over the figures and into the deep, open space on the right. If we examine a similar but reversed composition by Corot **(Fig. D),** we find our visual journey through the picture to be quite different. Now we tend to move from the background to the foreground, again from left to right. It is with some effort that we move back again into the deep space. The forms on the right seem to block a natural flow from left to right. A composition that is more heavily

C

D

weighted on the right will often feel denser, more closed, and the eye will seem to move against a visual current.

Sometimes artists use this current to create movement in an image or to stop it. On other occasions the artist looks for means to counteract the inequality of left and right. In the letterhead in **Fig. E,** a strong left to right flow is created by the long horizontal format, by the type which we read from left to right, and by the eye's tendency to scan in that direction. The momentum generated by this movement might cause our eyes to slide off the right-hand edge, but instead that momentum is gently slowed down and arrested by the progressive turning in of the figures on the right side. Their left-facing direction turns our eyes back into the image much in the same way that Corot's hill does.

Also see: Isometric Perspective, p. 84
Unenclosed Space, p. 96

A

RUDOLF ARNHEIM
FILM AS ART

ff

B

C

The Center

EVERY field has a center, sometimes easy to see and sometimes not. In a square or rectangle, the center is where the two diagonals cross; in a circle, it is the point where radii come together. In an irregular field a more complex interaction of forces determines the center, and we may have to look and "feel" more tentatively with our eyes before we can decide where the center seems to be. You could, of course, find the physical balance point of an irregular flat shape by cutting the shape out of stiff cardboard and balancing it on the tip of a finger. This will show you the geometric center or center of gravity, but the *visual* center is not necessarily the same **(Fig. A)**.

In a rectangular field, for example, the point at which an element will feel comfortably centered to the eye is usually a little *above* the midpoint. In Pentagram's design for a book cover **(Fig. B)** the central form is placed slightly above the halfway mark so that it does not look low in the rectangle. This is an example of visual centering.

The center of any visual field is the most potent area of the design. An element placed at the center of a page or canvas is highlighted and has a greater visual impact or force. Often a small element placed at the center of a composition becomes the most important element. Even when left empty, the center remains a visual magnet, exerting its pull on the forms around it.

In another sense, each shape or group of shapes in a visual field forms its own center. Like planets in a solar system, each shape has its own attraction for the eye, and these subcenters compete with each other and with the visual center for importance. The sum of all these competing forces is what we call composition.

When Degas places an open book at the center of a composition **(Fig. C),** it becomes an actor at least as important as the man and woman who flank it. Even though it is a relatively blank form, without the visual interest and weight that the surrounding heads and hands have, it becomes the dominant element in the composition.

Jean Hélion uses two competing centers in his "Circular Tensions" **(Fig. D).** Four black vertical lines extend downward and end exactly at the horizontal midpoint of the square canvas. The gap bracketed by the two central lines marks the vertical midpoint. The center of the field having been established, a second, "off-center" center is set up, implied by the circular arcs that seem to surround it. A tug of war is set up between these two forceful centers, and the visual tension that results becomes the theme of the work.

Figure B. Pentagram Design, book cover, "Film as Art." (Courtesy of Pentagram Design, London)

Figure C. Edgar Dégas, "Violinist and Young Woman." c. 1871. (The Detroit Institute of Arts; Bequest of Robert H. Tannahill, No. 70.167)

Figure D. Jean Hélion, "Circular Tensions." 1931–1932. (Center for Art and Communication; Vaduz, Liechtenstein)

D

Also see: Top & Bottom, p. 48
Symmetry, p. 22

The Edge

We tend to notice forms placed close to or at the edges of a composition. As a shape or a line comes closer to the edge, visual tension increases, a viselike "closing of the gap" as form and edge come together **(Fig. A)**.

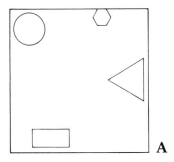

A

The special "electricity" of the edge has led some artists to work close to these boundaries as an interesting alternative to placing things in the center of their compositions. Edward Weston's photograph "Portrait of Neil" **(Fig. B)** uses the edge in this active way. The camera's viewfinder crops the torso and encloses it in a tight rectangle. The narrow black spaces to the left and right seem to pulse and caress the almost transparent and ghostly torso. The edge of the frame forms a contrasting straight line against which the gentle in and out movement of the edge of the torso can be easily seen.

The poster by Frances Butler in **Fig. C** also emphasizes the edge by placing most of the visual action away from the center. A sort of visual centrifugal force results. Blocks of type, tex-

B

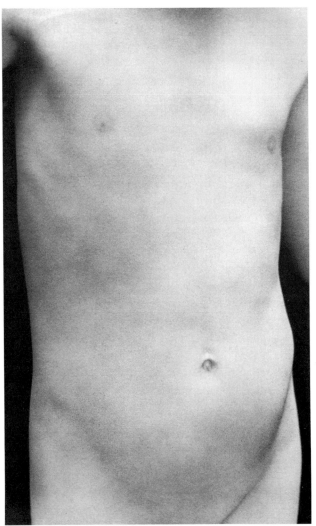

C

tured edges, and shape and size changes press outward toward the edges, leaving a central zone to be filled with color.

Paying careful attention to the border of a composition emphasizes the limitation of the frame and the self-contained quality of an image. It tends to make us even more aware that all the forms refer back to one another rather than establishing relationships with shapes and objects outside the two-dimensional field.

In a composition like Vallotton's street scene in **Fig. D,** forms seem rather casually to ignore the edge as a containing force. Shapes poke right through the boundaries of the rectangle, implying that space continues beyond the edge. The cropping creates new shapes out of, for example, the predictable hourglass silhouette of the black dress, and the relatively empty center of the composition contains an airiness and a generosity of space that reminds us of both the business and the large scale of urban space.

Also see: Tension, p. 20
Top & Bottom, p. 48
Unenclosed Space, p. 96
Scale/Size Relationships, p. 108

Figure B. Edward Weston, ''Neil, Nude.'' 1925. (Collection, The Museum of Modern Art, New York; © 1981 Arizona Board of Regents, Center for Creative Photography)

Figure C. Frances Butler, ''Colored Reading.'' (Courtesy Frances Butler, Berkeley, Calif.)

Figure D. Felix Vallotton, ''A Street in Paris.'' (The Metropolitan Museum of Art, New York; Robert Lehman Collection, 1975)

D

The Picture Plane

I N this chapter we have been assuming that we are looking at a flat, two-dimensional surface onto which we can put flat shapes, draw lines and marks, move from top to bottom, left to right, and so on. Even though the forms may look three-dimensional, they are organized in terms of what is called the *picture plane*, the frontal plane or actual surface upon which we work.

The picture plane and the characteristic of flatness cannot be ignored, but the role given to this plane in a work of art can vary considerably. An artist can treat the surface as just that, a flat field on which to serve up flat elements. At the other extreme, an artist can create a feeling of depth, only implying that the surface, like a glass wall, is there. The painting by David Hockney in **Fig. A** pokes fun at this traditional Renaissance painter's way of perceiving the picture plane. Hockney's figure exists in a three-dimensional space "box" and reminds us of the picture plane through an old, familiar sight gag.

Cubist painting marked a startling shift in emphasis in the treatment of the picture surface. Western artists had for hundreds of years stressed a feeling of depth in painting. Al-

Figure A. David Hockney, "A Play within a Play." 1963. (Courtesy David Hockney, London)

Figure B. Pablo Picasso, "Still Life." 1918. (National Gallery of Art, Washington; Chester Dale Collection)

Figure C. Jean-Baptiste-Simeon Chardin, "Fruit, Jug, and a Glass." c. 1755. (National Gallery of Art, Washington; Chester Dale Collection)

A

though they paid close attention to the arrangement of forms on the surface, the surface itself was more hinted at than actually present. In Cubist painting the surface became explicit, and Cubist influenced pictures tend to look flatter than, say, Impressionist or Old Master paintings. In contrast to the roundness and generosity of space in the painting by Chardin **(Fig. C),** the forms in the Cubist painting by Picasso **(Fig. B)** seem to be pressed against that sheet of glass, the picture plane humorously referred to in Hockney's painting.

There are smaller, interior planes that we see ''behind'' the frontal plane. These planes

B

C

may be parallel to the picture plane, echoing it, or they may sit at an angle to it, thrusting in and out of the picture. Interior planes may be straight or curved, may be created by the surfaces of objects in a still life or by diagonal shapes, parallel lines, or the construction lines of perspective. This structure of interior planes, which can act out a spatial play behind the curtain formed by the picture plane, is nevertheless always perceived in relation to it **(Fig. D).**

In some forms of visual art the flat frontal plane has historically had primary importance. **Fig. E,** a page of classical typography, is a beautiful example of the ''flat page'' tradition of type design and layout used to create unity, elegance, and order. Some modern typographers, by contrast, have broken with tradition and created more complex interaction between the flat-

ter vocabulary of letter forms and the spatial possibilities of the page **(Fig. F),** but even when typographers dig deep into the picture space, it is always with regard for the special rules of the surface plane.

Also see: Space Cues: Isometric Perspective, p. 84
Space: The Pictorial Box, p. 86

Figure D. Joseph Stella, ''Brooklyn Bridge.'' 1917–1918. (Yale University Art Gallery; Gift of Collection Societe Anonyme)

Figure E. Ashendene Press, Pages from ''Les Amours Pastorales de Daphnis et Chloé.'' Published in London, 1931.

Figure F. Herbert Bayer, Samples of Bayer Type. 1934. (The Fogg Museum, Harvard University, Cambridge; Gift of Josef Albers)

D

Ce qu'il dit
à Chloé

controuva qu'il avoit arraché des serres mêmes de l'aigle l'oison de Lycenion; puis, l'embrassant, la baisa comme Lycenion l'avoit baisé durant le déduit, car cela seul lui pouvoit-il, à son avis, faire sans danger; et Chloé lui mit sur la tête le chapelet qu'elle avoit fait, et en même temps lui baisoit les cheveux, comme sentant à son gré meilleur que les violettes, puis lui donna de sa panetière à repaître du raisin sec et quelques pains, et souventefois lui prenoit de la bouche un morceau, et le mangeoit elle, comme petits oiseaux prennent la becquée du bec de leur mère.

Ainsi qu'ils mangeoient ensemble, ayant moins de souci de manger que de s'entrebaiser, une barque de pêcheurs parut, qui voguoit au long de la côte. Il ne faisoit vent quelconque, et étoit la mer fort calme, au moyen de quoi ils alloient à rames; et ramoient à la plus grande diligence qu'ils pouvoient, pour porter en quelque riche maison de la ville leur poisson tout frais pêché; et ce que tous mariniers ont accoutumé de faire pour alléger leur travail, ceux-ci le

La chanson
des mariniers

faisoient alors; c'est que l'un deux chantoit une chanson marine, dont la cadence régloit le mouvement des rames, et les autres, de même qu'en un chœur de musique, unissoient par intervalles

104

garderoient à leur propre fils. Car non-guères auparavant leur étoit né un petit garçon. Et Dryas lui-même quelquefois se laissoit aller à ces raisons; aussi que chacun lui faisoit des offres bien au-delà de ce que méritoit une simple bergère; mais considérant puis après que la fille n'étoit pas née pour s'allier en paysannerie, et que s'il arrivoit qu'un jour elle retrouvât sa famille, elle les feroit tous heureux, il différoit toujours d'en rendre certaine réponse, et les remettoit d'une saison à l'autre, dont lui venoit à lui cependant tout plein de présents qu'on lui faisoit.

CE que Chloé entendant en étoit fort déplaisante, et toutefois fut long-temps sans vouloir dire à Daphnis la cause de son ennui. Mais voyant qu'il l'en pressoit et importunoit souvent, et s'ennuyoit plus de n'en rien savoir qu'il n'auroit pu faire après l'avoir su, elle lui conta tout: combien ils étoient de poursuivants qui la demandoient, combien riches! les paroles que disoit Napé à celle fin de la faire accorder, et comment Dryas n'y avoit point contredit, mais remettoit le tout aux prochaines vendanges. Daphnis oyant telles nouvelles, à peine qu'il ne perdît sens et entendement, et se séant à terre, se prit à pleurer, disant qu'il mourroit si Chloé

invente des pré-
textes pour dif-
férer sa réponse

Chloé, ennuyée,
dit tout à son
amant,

109

Grouping

Grouping is one of the techniques employed by artists to organize and structure pieces of visual information into graspable visual patterns. Our visual mechanism does this organizing unconsciously, whether we want it to or not. We will see pieces of a design as members of a group when they share a similar shape, color, value, or orientation in space. We also group by proximity: when forms are close together, we may see them as belonging to the same group even if the forms themselves are different **(Fig. A).**

We can see this principle at work by looking at Botticelli's ''The Adoration of the Magi'' **(Fig. B).** We notice first of all how the two bunches of figures to the right and left of the center form tight groups, and how each of these groups creates a sort of crescent shape. Although each figure is defined by a clear outline, each is perceived in terms of the larger containing shape. The right-hand crescent both points to and is echoed by the shape formed by the Virgin and Child. This repetition causes us to read yet another group, and makes a visual echo between these elements of the picture. A series of vertical elements—architecture, trees, and the vertical folds of hanging drapery on several figures—also read as a group which unifies different levels of space as well as right and left. This happens again as we notice the visual connection between the round, draped shoulders of the worshippers and the round forms of the horses on the right. Grouping keeps making connections of these kinds over and over throughout the picture, helping to bring its many parts together into a clear visual whole.

Piet Zwart's type layout in **Fig. C** also uses grouping to create visual connections that extend across the page. The lines group by direc-

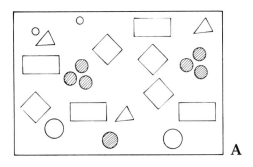

A

B

tion, with diagonals in one group, and verticals in another. Circular forms make another group, while individual letters above and below the large "O" make a squarish constellation that holds the "O" in place.

In the painting by Georges Braque **(Fig. D)** grouping is used to break up the usual relationships between objects and to create connections based on light and dark shapes. The still-life objects are arranged in a circular composition on the tabletop, but another group of dark shapes form a scattered constellation of their own across the surface of the design. The white shapes, in turn, form their own family. Objects such as the book or wine glass are members of both groups.

Also see: Gestalt, p. 6

Hierarchy & Subdivision, p. 28

Figure B. Sandro Botticelli, "The Adoration of the Magi." early 1480s. (National Gallery of Art, Washington; Andrew W. Mellon Collection)

Figure C. Piet Zwart, "Hot spots irrevocably lead to a blown fuse / Protect your cable network by N.K.F. cable / Dutch cable factory Delft." 1926. (Collection, The Museum of Modern Art, New York; Gift of Philip Johnson)

Figure D. Georges Braque, "Still Life with Grapes." 1927. (The Phillips Collection, Washington, D.C.)

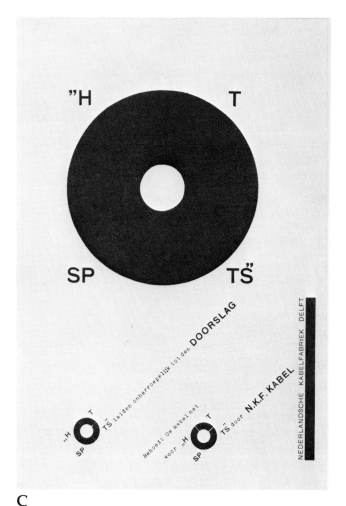

C

D

Mark Making

A

A mark made with a brush, pencil, or any other tool is a surprisingly important element in a work of visual art. The soft, wet blob of paint made by a heavily loaded brush, the hairline of an etching needle, the pointed comma produced by a sharpened pencil, though simple and easily made, can become the basic units of complex visual structures. Just as many units of square tiles can be put together in a mosaic to produce complex patterns, so can a simple mark be used as a visual building block. Simple marks can be combined into groups and can change color, orientation in space, and position in the composition. This handful of possibilities becomes the framework within which the artist invents and creates.

Jasper Johns used a straight painted stroke as the basic building unit in his painting in **Fig. A.** The mark is clearly handmade. When a mark is large enough to be read as a real and physical thing, we are reminded that the surface itself is an object, a flat area with paint on it, as well as being a window onto an illusionistic space. A mark used in this way tends to draw the eye to the surface, and works of art in which an emphasis on the surface is important often use a highly visible mark.

One of the qualities of such media as oil paint or clay is their ability to preserve the smallest and most fleeting traces of the maker's hand. This sense of an intimate, silent, but palpable physical presence can make a 2000-year-old painting seem as fresh and lively as if it were still wet. This quality has the effect, as the critic John Berger pointed out, of "closing the gap" between the viewer and the work of art, which may come to us across the space of centuries.

The variety, flexibility, and even quirkiness of a handmade mark were a focus for artists like the American painter Charles Burchfield, whose repertoire of different marks, long strokes, short touches, and curved, jagged, and straight strokes become primary tools **(Fig. B).**

In some forms of visual art, the visible mark of the hand at work is eliminated. In the mechanical reproduction of books and magazines, in tightly rendered precisionist painting, in much graphic design, the cooler, more impersonal look of paint applied precisely in smooth layers is preferred. Here the hand of the artist might interfere with a perfect illusion of form or with the unified texture of a smoothly polished surface **(Fig. C).**

In Roy Lichtenstein's painting in **Fig. D** the tiny dots of color used in magazine and newspaper reproduction, the small strokes and hatch marks that create light and shade in the repertoire of realism and illusionism, are magnified

B

C

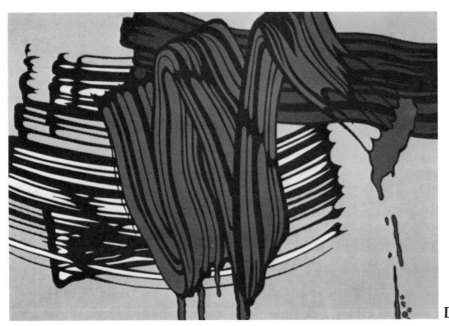

D

until each mark becomes an easily visible shape sitting on the surface. It is as if the artist wanted to confront the viewer with the paradox that art is, in one sense, ''just lines on paper'' while taking exceptional pleasure in seeing all of the effects, from transparency to reflection to light and shadow, that marks can produce.

Also see: Materials & Line Qualities, p. 142

Light Cues: Value, p. 170

Color Making Light, p. 216

Realism & Abstraction, p. 240

Figure A. Jasper Johns, ''Between the Clock and the Bed.'' 1981. (Collection, The Museum of Modern Art, New York; Given anonymously)

Figure B. Charles Birchfield, ''Dandelions, Seed Balls, and Trees.'' 1917. (The Metropolitan Museum of Art, New York; Arthur Hoppock Hearn Fund, 1940)

Figure C. Fernand Léger, ''Nude on a Red Background.'' 1927. (Hirshhorn Museum and Sculpture Garden, Smithsonian Institution; Gift of Joseph J. Hirshhorn Foundation, 1972)

Figure D. Roy Lichtenstein, ''Big Painting (#6).'' 1965. (Private collection)

Texture

A visual texture is a tactile quality that evokes our sense of touch through our eyes alone. There is obviously a difference between illusions of texture made entirely of marks drawn on paper and a texture that really can be felt with the hand. Fur, fabric, or the rough surface of tree bark look to the eye as rough as they feel to the touch, but in a photograph we are able to experience texture only with the sense of sight **(Fig. A)**.

Texture creates visual weight. Visual texture is useful in helping us ''feel'' the solidity, roundness, or heaviness of a form. A textured surface may feel slow to the eye, clogged, or difficult to move across and can invite a slower, more focused examination of forms, as opposed to the quickness of a smooth, polished surface. Realists, like the Dutch painters of the seventeenth century, painted richly textured objects and lovingly depicted their surfaces in an effort to emphasize the weight and material solidity of the subject **(Fig. B)**.

Other artists have focused on the texture of the paint itself, juxtaposing its reality with the illusion of the picture space. In this case the texture recalls both the two dimensionality of a picture, and the physical, seductive beauty of the paint itself **(Fig. C)**.

When we experience one sense through another, in this case touch through sight, we experience imaginatively. We need not think of visual texture as being only an alternative way of experiencing a particular sensation. When we look at a page of type and see a variety of sizes, weights, and densities of text, our perception is akin to that of running our fingers over various surfaces—coarse, smooth, rubbly, scratchy **(Fig. D)**. Our eyes move quickly and slowly, easily

A

B

and with difficulty, over the different blocks of type. Here texture is a visual element, more like color or value, which lends a beautiful richness and variety without destroying the unified organization of a very complicated page.

Also see: Packed Space, p. 98

Microstructure/Macrostructure, p. 110

Figure A. Massimo Vignelli, ''XXXII Biennale/Internazionale/D'arte Venezia/32B.'' 1964. (Massimo Vignelli, Vignelli Associates, New York)

Figure B. Abraham van Beyeren, ''Still Life with a Silver Wine Jar and a Reflected Portrait of the Artist.'' 1655. (The Cleveland Museum of Art; Mr. and Mrs. William H. Marlatt Fund)

Figure C. Francis Bacon, ''Study for Portrait of Van Gogh III.'' 1957. (Hirshhorn Museum and Sculpture Garden, Smithsonian Institution; Gift of Joseph H. Hirshhorn Foundation, 1966)

Figure D. Herb Lubalin, Type specimen from ''U & lc.'' 1978. (Courtesy Herb Lubalin Study Center of Design and Typography, The Cooper Union, New York)

C

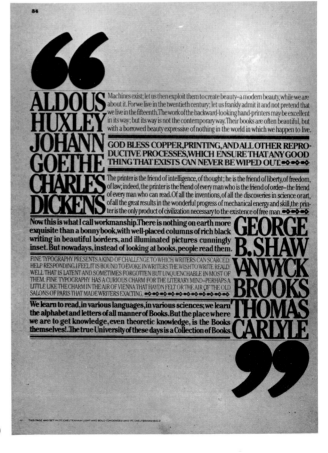

D

Lu Chi, ''Autumn Landscape with Herons and Ducks.'' (The Metropolitan Museum of Art; Dorothy Graham Bennett Fund, 1980)

Space

4

Introduction

W HEN we examined "flatness" we saw that a page or surface is perceived differently than is the world around us. We saw some of the ways in which shapes, lines, and values behave and interact on a two-dimensional surface. The same guidelines for visual organization are followed in all types of art, regardless of the purpose, the culture, the style, or the media. The late twentieth-century typographer and the eighteenth-century Japanese printmaker both may place a shape within an enclosed visual field in similar ways.

There is a second, complementary way of thinking about the surface. The flat surface has what an artist once termed "a mysterious desire to contain spaces, objects, and forms." We look for depth, a feeling of three-dimensionality, in any flat design whether it depicts three-dimensional objects or not. This sensation of space is at the heart of the visual arts, whether in a re- alistic rendering of observed objects **(Fig. A)** or in the manipulation of nonfigurative shapes.

There seems to be a contradiction in the notion that we can choose between two different ways of looking at the same thing. Should we see flat, or should we look for depth? In fact, the two go together, and in two-dimensional art we can't have one without the other. As we will see, the three-dimensional illusion is inevitable in two-dimensional images, as is the fact of their flatness. It is the job of the artist to control and relate the forces of depth and surface and to use both to advantage.

The three-dimensional effect that we see in so much visual art is obtained by the careful organization and manipulation of flatness. Artists see space by looking carefully at the surface.

Figure A. Engraving after Gustave Doré, ''Over London by Rail.'' 1872.

A

Figure/Ground

T HE smallest mark, placed on a sheet of paper, will create a sensation of space. Try it. Place a dot on a page, and you will see either a dot floating in front of a large empty space, or the solid surface of the page with a small hole in it revealing a darker layer beneath.

The most basic illusion creates a very simple kind of space: one thing in front of another. We call this interaction of shape and field a *figure/ground relationship*. *Figure* is the shape "in front of" the *ground* on which it appears to sit. The relationship may also be referred to as *foreground* and *background*. What we know about depth and distance in the real world enables us to "read" this space in a realistic image. For example, in the print in **Fig. A,** the lower zone reads as foreground, while other parts of the picture, the great mass at the left and the small shapes on the right, seem to be further away, creating middle and background. The relationship is less clear-cut in a work of art that deals with a nonrealistic space. In the painting by Jean Hélion **(Fig. B)** the sense of one thing in front of another is created by the way we read shape, color, texture, and other formal qualities. Whether the work is representational or not, artists must know how to control figure/ground relationships, to make one area read as figure while another reads as ground. The artist will also want to vary the figure/ground rhythm to create open and closed spaces in a composition.

Figure shapes and ground shapes each have their own particular characteristics and play different roles in a visual configuration. Generally, a figure area looks visually heavy and self-contained, a *positive* shape or area. A

A

ground, on the other hand, tends to look empty, *negative*, visually lighter, or less loaded **(Fig. C)**. We could say that the figure is the main visual event (the actor) and the ground is a supporting element (the stage). Figure areas tend to be mobile looking, while grounds seem to be stable. The actor, in other words, moves across the stage; the stage does not move around the actor. Still, in any theater, the stage, even when it is bare, is an integral, critical part of the drama.

Also see: Hierarchy & Subdivision, p. 28

Figure A. Edgar Degas, ''The Road (La Route).'' c. 1878–1880. (National Gallery of Art, Washington; Rosenwald Collection)

Figure B. Jean Hélion, ''Standing Figure.'' 1935. (Albright-Knox Art Gallery, Buffalo, New York; Room of Contemporary Art Fund, 1944)

B

C

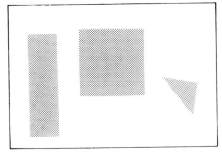

Figure/Ground Strategies

How can we make one shape in a design read as "figure" and another part become "ground"? There are several possible strategies available for controlling this relationship.

Convex shapes, those whose boundaries curve outward, tend to be seen as figure, whereas concave shapes, those with boundaries bending inward, tend to be read as ground areas **(Fig. A)**.

Figure is also created by texture. Textured areas are generally seen as positive shapes, whereas a lack of texture creates the visual emptiness of a ground. In **Fig. B** areas become solid looking or empty looking as texture is applied.

Value and color also affect our reading of figure and ground. More contrast of color or value usually results in a stronger separation of figure and ground. In general, a darker value or more brilliant color appears to be visually heavier and more positive than does a lighter or duller color **(Fig. C)**.

Lines that are close together will visually attract one another and create a more positive or full-looking space between them, a figure quality. As lines move further apart, the space

between them becomes emptier and less compact **(Fig. D)**.

It is, of course, not necessary for us to assume, as the diagrams here do, that a single element (texture, or line, or value) will be used to create a figure/ground relationship. Most visual images combine several of these elements, so that the force of one may counterbalance the tendencies of another.

Henri Matisse's collage "Venus" **(Fig. E)** demonstrates how powerfully these figure/ground strategies affect our perception of two-dimensional images. Here the shapes that are figure in the literal sense, the dark paper painted and glued onto the white page, become, for our eyes, ground shapes against which we see the image of a nude, her form made of a convex shape, its edges drawing together to create a full, swelling volume. The cut paper shapes, their dark and brilliant blue animated by the texture of visible brushstrokes, still retain enough figural quality to make for a lively exchange between these two sets of shapes, competing for the front of the picture space.

In **Fig. F** we see the background taking on a strong figure quality by virtue of its dark value

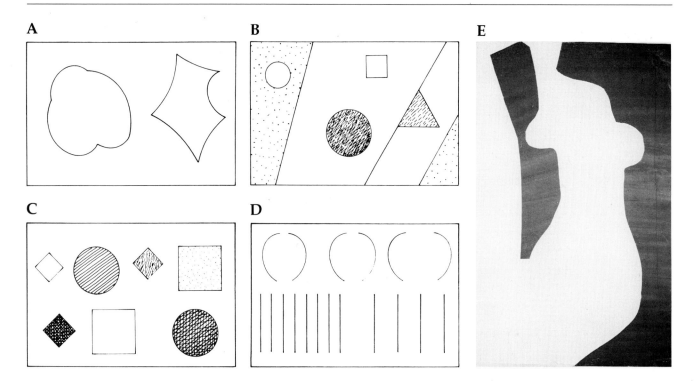

A

B

C

D

E

and texture in the form of a regular pattern. The two caped women appear almost as holes in the background, but they regain some figure quality as a result of their irregular and convex shapes and the details of holly, facial features, and so forth which suggest some volume. The reading of the background as figure is so strong that even the bands of type at top and bottom appear to be slightly behind the patterned rectangle.

Gustav Klimt used a varied sequence of figure/ground relationships to create a rhythm of open/closed, positive/negative, empty/full areas in his composition **(Fig. G).** Notice that as an area becomes more textured, its visual weight as well as its figure quality increases. In the central area, a positive shape is created by the gently swelling convex outline, but a feeling of emptiness is created also, by the looser, more scat-

tered texture. The areas with the least noticeable textures, the zones to the left and right, read as empty space or background.

Also see: Texture, p. 64
Positive/Negative Shape, p. 124
Value Creating Depth, p. 180
Color Space, p. 218

Figure E. Henri Matisse, ''Venus.'' 1952. (National Gallery of Art, Washington; Ailsa Mellon Bruce Fund)

Figure F. Will Bradley, ''The Inland Printer Christmas.'' 1895. (Collection, The Museum of Modern Art, New York; Gift of Joseph H. Heil)

Figure G. Gustav Klimt, ''Hope II.'' 1907–1908. (Collection, The Museum of Modern Art, New York; Mr. and Mrs. Ronald S. Lauder and Helen Acheson Funds, and Serge Sabarsky)

F

G

Space Cues: Gradients

A

B

THERE are a handful of strategies for creating a feeling of depth or space, simple cues that tell the viewer that a particular area of a two-dimensional composition is to be read three dimensionally. Used alone or in combination, these signals can create the most refined and sophisticated sensations of depth and volume on a surface.

A *gradient* is a gradual, orderly, step-by-step *change* in some visual quality. It might be the change from darker to lighter gray in a scale, or the swelling and tapering of an oval, or a change from large forms to medium-sized to small ones.

Gradients are effective tools for creating pictorial space. A gradual size change from large to small, for example, can create a series of clear visual steps into the picture space. This kind of gradient is used in Hendrick Avercamp's scene in **Fig. A.** The diminishing sizes of the skaters against the expanse of ice become stepping-stones toward a distant horizon in the picture. Perspective systems formalize this gradient of size change.

To be effective, the visual change in a gradient must happen in a series of steps. There

C

must be enough steps so that the eye does not have to jump, and the intervals between them must form a reasonably smooth progression. When there is a change from foreground to background without an adequate number of steps in between, we tend to see a small form next to a large one, instead of a distant and near form. This kind of flattening of space can be seen in Toulouse-Lautrec's poster for Jane Avril **(Fig. B).**

A classic and very effective gradient can be seen in Moholy-Nagy's design in **Fig. C.** The letters, a gradient of large to small, break the flat surface with an inward motion, creating depth.

Figure A. Hendrick Avercamp, ''A Scene on the Ice.'' c. 1625. (National Gallery of Art, Washington; Ailsa Mellon Bruce Fund)

Figure B. Henri de Toulouse-Lautrec, ''Jane Avril: Jardin de Paris.'' 1893. (Collection, The Museum of Modern Art, New York; Gift of A. Conger Goodyear)

Figure C. Laszlo Moholy-Nagy, ''Poster (Photomontage).'' 1923. (Photograph courtesy, The Museum of Modern Art, New York)

Also see: Diagonal Recession, p. 90
Gradients & Movement, p. 158
Stroboscopic Motion, p. 162
Value Creating Depth, p. 180
Volume Color/Film Color, p. 224

Space Cues: Overlap

PERHAPS the most elementary of the space cues is overlap, the illusion of one shape seeming to interrupt or block our view of another **(Fig. A)**.

In **Fig. B,** a small Indian painting, overlapping is about the only means we are given to read our way from foreground to background. The outline of each figure tends to be smooth and unbroken, and the figures in the background are not smaller than those in front, as they would be in a perspective drawing. Here overlapping allows us to untangle what might otherwise be visually ambiguous. By allowing our eye to ''walk'' through the crowd, overlapping keeps a shallow, packed space from becoming flat.

In the textile in **Fig. C**, overlapping is avoided, and the image does appear to be rather flat. Here, although a deep space is depicted, we are given very few space cues for a three-dimensional reading. Our eyes move up and down the surface, but we have difficulty seeing one thing in front of another. The forms appear to be pressed flat between two sheets of glass.

In contrast, the space in Degas' painting **(Fig. D)** is generous, with a feeling of air and space around each form. In this case, overlap helps to organize a more open space. The light hat overlaps the edge of the table and the hanging ribbon, clearly putting it in front of the group of hats on stands. They, in turn, overlap the woman's head and shoulder, locating her in the middle distance, and so on. By reading each form behind the one overlapping, we pick out a path in which to travel through a space that is comfortable and in which forms are held in place despite the absence of horizontals anchoring forms to the floor.

B

C

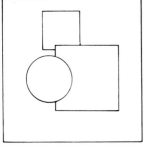

A

In El Lissitzky's "Proun 3 A" **(Fig. E)** overlap is used in a slightly different way. Here every form overlaps or is overlapped by another, but the overlaps tend to be either total, one shape completely enclosed within another, or else so slight that we are just able to discern the spatial order of shapes at their edges, such as in the way the white square barely overlaps the dark crescent and the middle-value square which flank it. By this means, Lissitzky creates a delicate, shallow, but unified space, while also retaining to a large degree the characteristic configuration of each shape—the squareness of the square, the even curve of a circle—with little distortion of their outlines.

Also see: Space & Flatness Together, p. 102

Figure B. Darbár of Jahanir, from a Jahangir-nama manuscript. Mughal School, c. 1620. (Courtesy, Museum of Fine Arts, Boston; Francis Bartlett Donation of 1912 and Picture Fund, 14.654)

Figure C. "Futonji." Okayama Prefecture, early 19th century. (Honolulu Academy of Arts; Purchase, 1937)

Figure D. Edgar Degas, "The Milliner's Shop." 1879–1884. (Mr. and Mrs. Lewis Larned Coburn Memorial Collection, 1933.428; © Art Institute of Chicago. All Rights Reserved.)

Figure E. El Lissitzky, "Proun 3A." c. 1920. (Los Angeles County Museum of Art; Purchased with funds provided by Mr. and Mrs. David E. Bright and the bequest of David E. Bright)

D

E

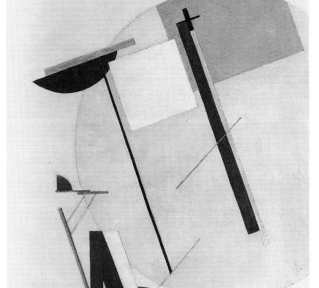

Space Cues: Size Change

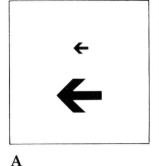

A

B

SIZE change is another basic tool used for creating a sense of space. When we see two similar objects of different sizes in a two-dimensional image, and we receive no visual information to the contrary, we tend to perceive that the larger one is near and the smaller one is far **(Fig. A)**.

A painting by Degas **(Fig. B)** relies heavily on size change to hollow out a background space. The field on which the horsemen are riding is rendered as a flat wall of tones. To carve depth and distance into this flatness, Degas uses a web of size comparisons from figure to figure to create the fragile space structure.

In another painting by Alex Katz **(Fig. C)** size changes are eliminated entirely, and space becomes curiously flattened. Here a lack of size difference results in a very shallow space, close to the picture plane, even while preserving the unbroken, clearly modeled and rounded form of realist painting.

Size change creates the visual action in the poster in **Fig. D.** The continuing variations in type size make a nonrealistic space that is strongly felt, that shifts rapidly from near to far to near again, and that has a complex and rhythmic structure.

Figure B. Edgar Degas, ''Race Horses at Longchamp.'' c. 1873–1875. (Courtesy, Museum of Fine Arts, Boston; S. A. Denio Collection. 03.1034)

Figure C. Alex Katz, ''Place.'' 1977. (Collection of Whitney Museum of American Art; Gift of Frances and Sydney Lewis. Acq. #78.23)

Figure D. Bruno Munari, ''Campari.'' 1965. (Collection, The Museum of Modern Art, New York; Gift of the designer)

Figure E. J. M. W. Turner, ''Mortlake Terrace.'' c. 1826. (National Gallery of Art, Washington; Andrew W. Mellon Collection)

An orderly size change in a gradient can create the most dramatic spatial illusions. When size change is gradual and in several even steps, our sense of pictorial space may be greatly enhanced. In the landscape by Turner **(Fig. E)** this orderly diminution of sizes gives us not merely a sense that a space exists, but a very clear and precise idea of distance and interval.

Also see: Space Cues: Gradients, p. 74
Scale/Size Relationships, p. 108

C

D

E

Space Cues: Vertical Location

Whenever we look at realist painting or photography, we usually expect the foreground to be in the lower part of the visual field and the forms in the distance to appear higher **(Fig. A).** Even without using perspective, artists sometimes manipulate space in accordance with this tendency to see the bottom of the field as near and the top as farther away.

Chinese painters were able to give an effect of large-scale space in long, thin vertical rectangles by using vertical location as a space cue. In the landscape in **Fig. B,** vertical location helps create a bird's-eye view in which small islands of landscape form climb back and up into the vast distance.

Man Ray's poster for the London Underground eliminates all space cues *except* vertical location to create a sense of infinite distance **(Fig. C).** Turn the poster upside down and notice the difference in the way you read the space. You are now likely to perceive the smaller form as nearer to the viewer.

Artists can also disrupt or reverse the expected relationships in order to produce fresh and unexpected pictorial spaces. To avoid the heavy, overloaded look that might result from placing all the foreground forms along the bottom of the canvas, Pieter Bruegel, in his painting "Hunters in the Snow" **(Fig. D),** designed a landscape space of hills and valleys that lifts up the foreground and pulls down the background. Foreground figures at the top of the hill are placed as high upon the canvas as background figures. The result is a space that seems both true to our sense of the way the world displays itself and satisfying as a design of symphonic richness, full of contrast, harmony, and movement.

Also see: Top & Bottom, p. 48

Figure B. Lu Chi, "Autumn Landscape with Herons and Ducks." c. 1488–1505. (The Metropolitan Museum of Art, New York; Dorothy Graham Bennett Fund, 1980)

Figure C. Man Ray, "Keeps London Going." 1932. (Collection, The Museum of Modern Art, New York; Gift of Bernard Davis)

Figure D. Pieter Bruegel, "Hunters in the Snow." 1565. (Kunsthistorisches Museum, Vienna)

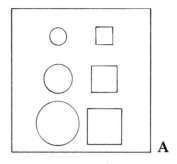

A

B

C

-KEEPS LONDON GOING

D

Space Cues: Vanishing Point Perspective

A

B

VANISHING point perspective is a set of rules for drawing which enables an artist to create an illusion of deep space on a two-dimensional surface. In this system the sizes of objects diminish in the distance and a unified and logical picture space can be described.

Although few artists today systematically study these rules of perspective drawing, we still look at visual art with an eye that has been conditioned by our past experience of art in which ''correct'' perspective *was* important.

The basic principle of vanishing point perspective is that lines that are parallel in the three-dimensional world are drawn on the two-dimensional page as converging lines that meet at one or more *vanishing points*. The angle of a line in relation to the vanishing point can make objects with geometric shapes (especially cubic forms) appear to sit nearer to or farther from the viewer **(Fig. A)**.

It is more difficult to use vanishing point perspective for forms that are not geometric and right angled, such as plants, human figures, or an oddly shaped rock. In the drawing by Luca Cambiaso **(Fig. B)** we sense the difficulty the artist had in trying to resolve the incompatibility of the fluid and curving forms of the figures with the geometry of a perspective construction. In general, vanishing point perspective works most effectively with what is sometimes called ''hard design,'' straightness and geometry, as opposed to ''soft design,'' irregular and organic form. In practice, the rules of vanishing point perspective construction must often be bent to accommodate nongeometric forms.

This kind of perspective forces us to see many different shapes in a single form. For example, a rectangular tabletop may become any one of the shapes shown in **Fig. C.** Thus this technique makes available to the artist a larger vocabulary of possible shapes.

With vanishing point perspective, an artist can put the viewer in a specific place, creating the impression that the picture is being viewed from one specific eye level and position.

The effect can be quite dramatic. In Piero della Francesca's ''Flagellation'' **(Fig. D)** the viewer sees the scene from a low eye level, looking up. The figures in the foreground loom up like the columns behind them. The violent theme of the picture is a distant event caught in a web of diagonals and vanishing points.

Part of what vanishing point perspective does is to set up an ''invisible'' gradient of size change, so that even when all the progressive steps from front to back are not visible, we can nevertheless perceive the progressive shrinking of sizes in depth.

In general, the use of vanishing point perspective tends to create more visual weight at the bottom of the picture plane. In most simple constructions of this type, the foreground, filled with larger forms, is at the bottom. As our eyes move up toward the top of the page, they are drawn toward the smaller forms of the background.

Artists have developed strategies to modify this built-in imbalance: tall forms in the foreground to ''fill'' the upper area of the picture plane, very large forms in the background, a low vanishing point or a strongly horizontal format, an empty foreground and a crowded distance, even a conscious distortion of sizes, would all tend to diminish the overloading of the bottom **(Fig. E).** Vanishing point perspective is one of the many systems in which what appears to be a limitation becomes instead a stimulus for inventive thinking.

Also see: Balance, p. 18

Top & Bottom, p. 48

Geometric/Organic Shape, p. 126

Gradients & Movement, p. 158

Figure A. Jan Vrederman De Vries, Plate from ''Perspective.'' 1604–1605.

Figure B. Luca Cambiaso, ''Martyrdom of St. Lawrence.'' Before 1581. (National Gallery of Art, Washington; Ailsa Mellon Bruce Fund)

Figure D. Piero della Francesca, ''The Flagellation.'' 1456–1457. (Galleria Nazionale delle Marches, Urbino)

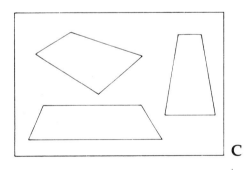

C

D

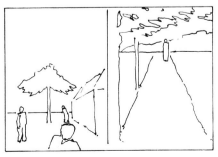

E

Space Cues: Isometric Perspective

I N contrast to the vanishing point perspective familiar to Western eyes, the perspective system most commonly found in Eastern art—that of China, Japan, and India—is *isometric perspective*, a linear perspective *without* a vanishing point, in which nothing gets smaller or larger.

Isometric perspective also favors straight edges and geometric forms, but its basic principle is that lines or edges that are parallel in nature *remain* parallel in the drawing. Lines do not come together in the distance. Thus its visual world feels entirely different from that of Western picture space **(Fig. A).** Objects appear to be always the same distance away from the viewer, whether they belong to the foreground, middle, or background. This ambiguity is often reinforced by a "flatness" in the painting itself, a lack of modeling, light and shade, and cast shadow, which is also characteristic of much Eastern art.

In **Fig. B** a large space is laid out, but the forms in the background are just as large as those much nearer. The idea of viewpoint is treated differently as well. Here, there is no single viewpoint. Instead, the viewer floats above the scene, seemingly able to see everywhere, equally well, at once. Therefore the space is infinite but also flatter looking; it seems to move forms sideways, through or across in a zig-zag as well as into the picture.

This "flatter" space allows for an easy interaction between the two-dimensional surface and the volumetric feeling of space by constantly acknowledging the flatness of the picture and returning the eye to the picture plane and the rhythms moving across it. For this reason, isometric perspective has been a preferred device of many modern artists as well as those graphic designers working in the tradition that emphasizes the surface over the deep space. The magical quality of isometric perspective is gracefully exploited by Milton Glaser in his poster in **Fig. C.** The image seems both deep and strangely flat; front and back reverse, and forms are drawn apart at the same time that they are pulled together.

Isometric perspective is also much used by architects, whose drawings must present a clear

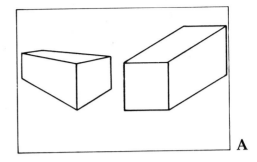

A

B

Figure B. "Battle of the Genji and the Heike." Japanese screen, detail. (The Metropolitan Museum of Art, New York; Rogers Fund, 1957)

Figure C. Milton Glaser, "One Print, One Painting." 1968. (Courtesy of the Library of Congress)

Figure D. John Hejduk, "Project A: House." 1967. (Courtesy of the artist)

---

overview of the sizes and positions of spaces, rooms, corridors, and so forth. The isometric system distorts shape less than does vanishing

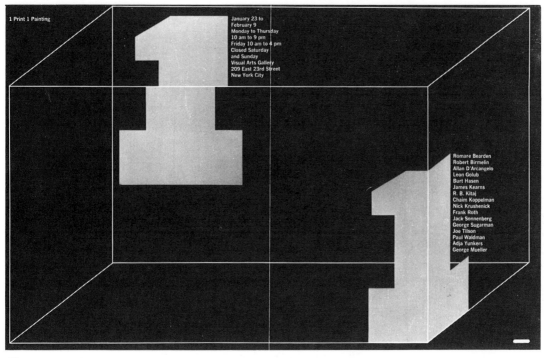

C

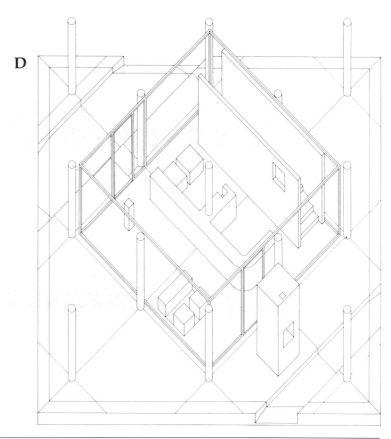

D

point perspective. An isometrically drawn cube keeps the parallelness of its edges; parallel lines do not become converging lines. Rooms of the same size stay the same size on paper, rather than getting smaller as they approach a vanishing point. The drawing by John Hejduk in **Fig. D** is an elegant example of a highly finished iso- metric architectural construction. It is also a beautiful and delicate composition in space.

Also see: The Picture Plane, p. 56

Unenclosed Space, p. 96

Flatness & Space Together, p. 102

The Pictorial Box

A

A surface to be drawn upon offers the potential for a whole range of three-dimensional spaces, from shallow, flattened layers to the deep space of aerial perspective. There is a need to organize the deep pictorial space that is created.

One way of organizing deep space in Western art is by imagining a *pictorial box*. **Fig. A,** a painting by Renaissance artist Antonello da Messina, is a good example. The picture surface is like a window or door through which we look to see open space on its other side. The artist, by stressing the "beginning" of the space, makes this door effect more obvious. He paints a stone doorway, its threshold (the threshold of the picture space) marked by a splendid pea-

cock, and then carefully works out a patterned floor which leads us inward to arrive finally at the walls which form the back, or outer limits of the space. The figure of St. Jerome is placed on a large, basically cube-shaped platform-study. The carpentered, right-angled feeling of the interior (so different from, for example, the space of an undulating landscape) is reinforced by the boxlike forms inside it.

The habit of seeing the picture surface as the front or doorway into a deeper space is one of the most familiar assumptions in the history of Western art, but despite its limitations, or because of them, the boxlike approach has been a useful tool for artists for hundreds of years. It is clear, with an easy-to-see front, top, bottom,

B

C

back, and sides. It is also controllable, a frame for space that can be as deep or as shallow as needed.

For example, the pictorial box in William Harnett's painting in **Fig. B** is so extremely shallow that it is hardly a space at all. The eye's movement into the space is stopped by a wall-like plane parallel to the picture surface, and the larger objects in the still life are wedged in parallel to these planes rather than shown in foreshortened views. What the pictorial box does best, however, is to draw the eye inward and create a kind of space that digs *into* the picture surface.

Space that penetrates the picture in this way is not limited to exact depictions of reality or perspective constructions. We find this kind of space in the work of artists like Louise Nev-

Figure A. Antonello da Messina, ''St. Jerome in His Study.'' c. 1475. (Reproduced by courtesy of the Trustees, The National Gallery, London)

Figure B. William Harnett, ''Old Models.'' 1892. (Courtesy, Museum of Fine Arts, Boston; The Hayden Collection, 39.761)

Figure C. Louise Nevelson, ''Black Wall.'' 1964. (Hirshhorn Museum and Sculpture Garden, Smithsonian Institution; Gift of Joseph H. Hirshhorn, 1966)

elson **(Fig. C),** which relies on the containing quality of the box (in this case, boxes) in which layers of form overlap and smaller elements are contained in spaces that have the intimate, enclosed feeling of the pictorial box.

Also see: The Picture Plane, p. 56

A

B

Frontal Recession

Sᴏᴍᴇᴛɪᴍᴇs pictorial space is created by a series of overlapping layers that are parallel to the picture plane, like cut-out, flat layers of stage scenery set parallel to the front of the stage. This way of moving into and through a space, sometimes called *frontal recession*, reminds the viewer of the flat surface even while leading the eye past it into the picture. Each layer of space echos the two-dimensional surface.

Figure A. William Bailey, ''Still Life with Rose Wall and Compote.'' (Hirshhorn Museum and Sculpture Garden, Smithsonian Institution; Gift of Mr. and Mrs. Robert Schoelkopf)

Figure B. Juan Gris, ''Fantomas.'' 1915. (National Gallery of Art, Washington; Chester Dale Collection)

Figure C. El Lissitzky, Cover design for ''Vesch/Gegenstand/Object.'' 1921–1922.

The still life in **Fig. A** is organized in this way. Almost every form is placed at a right angle to the picture surface, and an orderly stepping back is the central theme of the picture. This essentially flat way of presenting three-dimensional form is reinforced by the long horizontal of the table edge, placed parallel to the bottom edge of the canvas.

Juan Gris created a complex space out of shallow layers placed parallel to the frontal plane in his ''Still Life'' **(Fig. B).** The main forms are of colored rectangles and squares, their flatness reinforced by lettering which runs across the surface. The ''illusionistic'' wood graining of the large central rectangle, as literal as a sheet of veneer glued onto the painting, is a reminder that, on one level at least, the art of the Cubists was ''just paint on canvas.''

Frontal recession is a solution for artists who are organizing type which must remain legible, and so it is frequently used in graphic design. It is steady, stable and clear. Forms (or letters) on the same plane remain the same size, and we move back through space in orderly steps, as can be seen in El Lissitzky's bold and elegant page design **(Fig. C).** Although we read each block of type as existing on a different plane in space, some near, some farther away, we are most aware of the harmonious relationship they all share with the surface, and the extreme clarity of the text.

Also see: Space Cues: Overlap, p. 76

C

Diagonal Recession

A

WHEN the planes within a two-dimensional image are arranged so as to move into the picture space at an angle to the picture plane itself, the image tends to look more dynamic and have more movement. This moving back and forth in space, which we call *diagonal recession*, can be a visually dramatic and powerful tool.

Edouard Vuillard used diagonal recession to create visual excitement in what might otherwise be a static portrait. His image of an elderly man sitting in his study is dominated by a swirl of diagonal rectangles which thrust through the picture space, forming a carousel-like movement with the sitter at its hub **(Fig. A)**.

In George Bernard's photograph of Civil War ruins **(Fig. B)**, diagonal planes create a space that rushes toward the viewer and flees into the distance. An in and out rhythm is established as we read from left to right. The perspective of the arches draws the eye inward to the right and the brick mass of the chimney halts this inward movement and brings the eye back to the foreground.

B

When it is necessary to keep the flat feeling of the page, this kind of composition, with its violent ins and outs, is not as useful as frontal recession. It is used rather as a way of energizing space, creating a feeling of space that rushes along like a river.

Robert Cottingham arranges letter forms in diagonal recession in the painting in **Fig. C.** It could be argued that legibility is lessened to some degree, but the primary intent here is to arrange a striking image of form in space.

Also see: Left & Right, p. 50
Isometric Perspective, p. 84
Vertical/Horizontal/Diagonal, p. 160

Figure A. Edouard Vuillard, ''Théodore Duret.'' 1912. (National Gallery of Art, Washington; Chester Dale Collection)

Figure B. George Barnard, ''Ruins of the Railroad Depot, Charleston, South Carolina, 1864–65.'' Plate from *Photographic Views of Sherman's Campaign*. New York, 1866. (Collection, The Museum of Modern Art, New York; Acquired by exchange)

Figure C. Robert Cottingham, ''Buffalo Optical.'' 1982. (Collection, Birmingham Museum of Art, Birmingham, Alabama)

C

Space that Comes Out of the Picture Plane

RENAISSANCE artists dug into the picture plane, creating the illusion of distance *inside* the picture. Baroque artists began to change the emphasis, emphasizing movement toward or nearness to the viewer and creating spaces that related to the space *outside* the canvas in a way not seen before.

"St. Matthew and the Angel" by the Italian early Baroque painter Caravaggio **(Fig. A)** limits distance with an impenetrable black background, a solid wall of darkness that prevents the eye from probing deeply into the space. The "front" of the picture space is marked by a painted ledge at the bottom of the canvas. Caravaggio then moves forms beyond the front. The diagonally set wooden bench has one leg falling off the ledge, casting a shadow behind it as it moves toward the viewer, almost like a painted object in a trompe l'oeil painting.

This startling invasion of the viewer's space, with an impact like a fist thrusting out of the canvas, creates a visual drama that appeals to twentieth-century sensibilities as much as it did to seventeenth-century viewers. The poster by April Greiman and Jayme Odgers uses a similar kind of organization to move beyond the frontal plane **(Fig. B)**. As in the Caravaggio, movement into the picture is limited by a flat wall of color in front of which forms seem to fly through the air. Separate planes at the lower left and upper right break out of the framing rectangle, appearing to come off the surface of the page.

Another impressively forward-moving space is found in Mary Cassatt's "The Boating Party" **(Fig. C)**. There is an almost violent foreshortening in the angle of the rower's arm and right leg and in the sweeping curve of the boat's upper edge. The scene is set up as if viewed by a third party sitting in the bow of the boat which thrusts out of the picture into the viewer's space. The expanse of water, rather than being painted in a misty or atmospheric way, is more like a wall of deep blue, on top of which sits the opposite shore.

Also see: Value Contrast, p. 176
Color Space, p. 218
Realism & Abstraction, p. 240

Figure A. Michelangelo Caravaggio, "St. Matthew and the Angel." c. 1595. (Cheisa di S. Luigi dei Francesi, Rome)

Figure B. April Greiman and Jayme Odgers, "Academy of Television Arts and Sciences Student Television Awards, 1981." (Courtesy of April Greiman, Inc., Los Angeles)

Figure C. Mary Cassatt, "The Boating Party." 1893–1894. (National Gallery of Art, Washington; Chester Dale Collection)

A

B

C

Enclosed Space

ENCLOSED space, the sense of containment, has always had a special fascination for the viewer, with its overtones of mystery, its sense of the hidden and private.

Literal enclosure is the theme of Joseph Cornell's construction in **Fig. A.** The main enclosure, the box, is echoed and reechoed inside by smaller boxes, some of them containing maps which refer to landscape spaces, vast and unenclosed.

Enclosed space is also the theme of the painting by Jean-Honoré Fragonard in **Fig. B.** Here a leafy tunnel of trees cradles the tiny figures that give scale to the scene. The contrast between the airy, light-filled expanse of the upper half of the picture, and the shady alley of trees sharpens our sense of the difference between open and enclosed space.

Tina Modotti's ''Staircase'' **(Fig. C)** uses diagonals, light to dark gradients, and a composition that rotates like a snail shell around a center, to move the eye from larger foreground units to smaller background ones. Here, the sense of enclosure is created by the composition turning in upon itself.

In the Carolingian ornamental letter in **Fig. D** the sense of enclosure doesn't result from framing, as in the Cornell and the Fragonard, nor is there a centrifugal force like the one in the Modotti photograph which makes all the forms relate strongly to the center. Here the forms themselves seem to have a sense of the outer limits of the space, and they turn around as they reach it. This arabesque of lines and shapes, continually turning in upon itself, creates a strong sense of a composition that is self-contained, not held in by external forces.

Also see: Arabesque, p. 34
The Edge, p. 54
The Pictorial Box, p. 86
Size/Scale Relationships, p. 108

Figure A. Joseph Cornell, ''Object.'' 1942–1953. (Collection, The Museum of Modern Art, New York; Mr. and Mrs. Gerald Murphy Fund)

Figure B. Jean-Honoré Fragonard, ''A Shady Avenue.'' (The Metropolitan Museum of Art, New York; The Jules Bache Collection, 1949)

Figure C. Tina Modotti, ''Number 30/Staircase.'' c. 1923–1926. (Collection, The Museum of Modern Art, New York; Given anonymously)

Figure D. Incarnation initial from the ''Book of Kells.'' Early 9th century. (The Board of Trinity College, Dublin)

A

B

C

D

Unenclosed Space

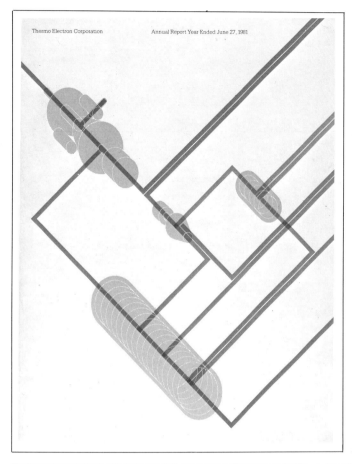

A

Visual elements can sometimes be organized to create a sense of unenclosed space, space that continues beyond the edges of the page.

Thomas Laidlaw and Michael Weymouth's cover design for an annual report effectively uses this kind of space to suggest a small slice of a much larger system **(Fig. A).** The edges of the page are deemphasized, while heavier dark bars powerfully lead the eye in from the left and off the page on the right. Unenclosed space encourages the viewer to imagine a larger world outside the page which complements and reinforces the visible material on the page.

The Japanese painted screen in **Fig. B** also describes an unenclosed picture space. The flowing stream moves through and across the picture and continues on its longer journey. This kind of open space is typical of much Oriental art and also typical of isometric perspective.

Both of these examples are essentially

Figure A. Thomas Laidlaw and Michael Weymouth, Annual report cover for Thermo Electron Corporation.

Figure B. Ogata Korin, ''Chrysanthemums by a Stream.'' (The Cleveland Museum of Art; Gift of Hanna Fund)

Figure C. Pieter Bruegel, ''The Harvesters.'' (The Metropolitan Museum of Art, New York; Rogers Fund, 1919)

Also see: Isometric Perspective, p. 84

unenclosed two-dimensional space, compositions of unbounded flatness. Pieter Bruegel's landscape in **Fig. C** is an unenclosed deep space, a generous three-dimensional construction of panoramic distance. The eye is able to travel, unobstructed, until the space dissolves into the infinite depths of the heat haze on the horizon. Rather than a pictorial box containing the three-dimensional structure of the picture, this is a strategy in which light encompasses all forms.

B

C

Packed Space

Some of the most effective and dramatic kinds of pictorial organization involve crowding the picture space with forms. When the picture space is "packed" with shapes, colors, and textures, a visual overload, an intensity or richness, can be achieved.

Kurt Schwitters' flyer for an evening of Dada poetry and performance is just such a packed space. The letterforms, jammed together on the page, create a visual image that captures the gleeful anarchy of an evening at a Surrealist nightclub **(Fig. A)**.

Alfonso Ossorio's work in **Fig. B** is also overloaded with form. The surface literally is covered: brightly colored three-dimensional objects are glued onto it. Form and color swirl together so that the surface seems to bubble with a festive and threatening intensity.

The tapestry in **Fig. C** uses a packed space to create an effect of visual sumptuousness. The crowd scene creates a feast of line, pattern, and color which, in its splendid and carefully worked out intricacies, would have been the fifteenth-century equivalent of a "technicolor" event.

In Leonard Dufresne's painting **(Fig. D)** the space is packed with forms that are swollen. What might have been inconsequential forms, like an ashtray or a doorknob, are transformed into important characters in the visual drama. Objects are eroticized and enlarged until they take on a physically and emotionally loaded presence. The most mundane objects have vitality in a space which seems to be burgeoning with volumes intent on filling every void.

In each of these examples, the artist has organized the space load in a particular way. Schwitters relies on a subtle vertical-horizontal grid which underlies the seemingly casual scattering of letterforms. Ossorio organizes large and smaller forms to create an even tension across the surface, a balance in which no single area becomes a center of attention. The tapestry maker uses a repeated vertical thrust on which smaller diagonals and patterns are hung, and a large diagonal from the executioner's hand to the severed head at lower right. Finally, Dufresne crowds the image with small islands or pockets of particular density or interest, so that we attentively examine the whole and the details, the space behind a door or inside a cabinet, with a focused intensity as we pick our way with slow deliberation through the picture space.

Also see: Texture, p. 64

Directed Tension, p. 156

Visual Information, p. 236

Figure A. Kurt Schwitters and Theo van Doesburg, "Kleine Dada Soiree." 1923.

Figure B. Alfonso Ossorio, "Between." 1963. (Collection of Whitney Museum of American Art; Gift of Howard and Jean Lipman. Acq. #65.95)

Figure C. "The Martyrdom of St. Paul" from the series *The Life of St. Peter.* c. 1460. (Courtesy, Museum of Fine Arts, Boston; Francis Bartlett Fund, 38.758)

Figure D. Leonard Dufresne, "The East Wind and the West Wind." 1985

A

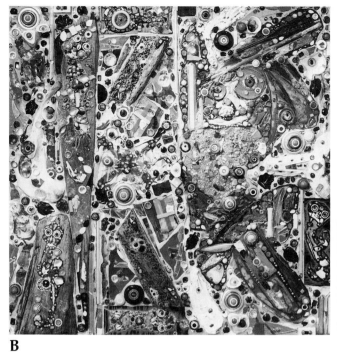

B

C

D

Empty Space

EMPTY space may seem like a nonquality, something that "isn't there," but dealing with it requires a knowledge of the visual field, an understanding of special properties and visual tensions built into different areas of the surface, and a sensitive and intuitive eye.

Emptiness is essential to the expression of the subject in David's "Death of Marat" (Fig. A). The upper part of the rectangle, conspicuously void of anything except the slight vibration of small, even brushstrokes, creates a visual silence which is, given that the subject is death, more eloquent than speech.

Alina Wheeler and Charles Menasion use emptiness in an entirely different way in their design in Fig. B. A generous white space creates a feeling of openness and airiness that reinforces the image of the flying kite. At the same time, the type and photographic elements are placed so that empty space is consciously shaped. The rectangle is carefully split by the diagonal kite string to form two facing, similarly shaped areas, and blocks of type are gracefully positioned to float, kitelike, across the page.

In the painting by Mark Rothko (Fig. C) the "empty" space is not empty at all, but rather a volume to be filled, not by objects but by light and color. Emptiness here allows color to speak without being laid over form. We see something akin to the space of the white page referred to earlier, but it is no longer blank.

Emptiness, then, can be as expressive as shape and form and can be used to express a wide range of ideas and emotions. The space left untouched in an image can be as important to its meaning as the objects that try to fill it.

Also see: Balance, p. 18
Mark Making, p. 62
The Shifting Edge, p. 148
Color Space, p. 218

Figure A. Jacques-Louis David, "Death of Marat." 1793. (Musées Royaux des Beaux-Arts de Belgique, Brussels)

Figure B. Alina Wheeler and Charles Menasion, Pennsylvania Hospital Annual Report Cover. 1982.

Figure C. Mark Rothko, "Blue, Orange, Red." 1961. (Hirshhorn Museum and Sculpture Garden, Smithsonian Institution; Gift of Joseph H. Hirshhorn Foundation, 1966)

A

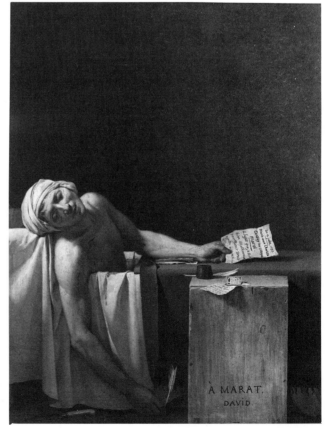

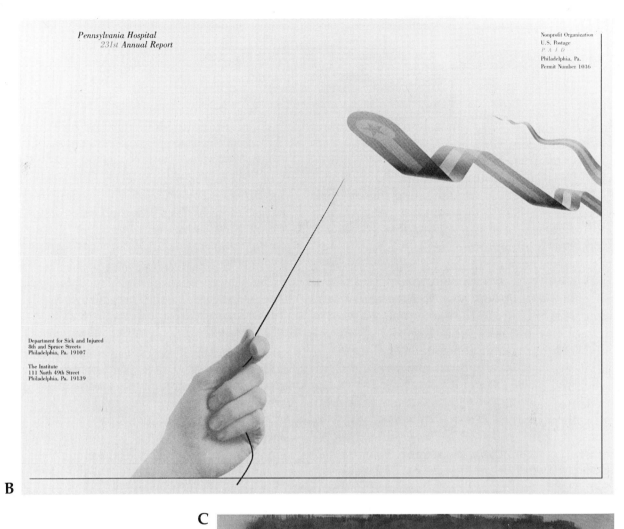

Pennsylvania Hospital
231st Annual Report

Nonprofit Organization
U.S. Postage
P A I D
Philadelphia, Pa.
Permit Number 1036

Department for Sick and Injured
8th and Spruce Streets
Philadelphia, Pa. 19107

The Institute
111 North 49th Street
Philadelphia, Pa. 19139

B

C

Flatness & Space Together

We design on a surface in two different and complementary ways. We can organize the imaginary space of the "pictorial box," creating a feeling of depth through size change, perspectives, shading, and so forth, and we can manipulate shapes on the flat surface, a field of forces that we subdivide into smaller areas of line, tone, and color.

Artists have recognized the need to demonstrate the best of both these visual worlds. For example, painters who have worked with a deep box of space have, at the same time, worked to arrange the surface. Sometimes doing this involves using three-dimensional elements to create two-dimensional movements across the surface of the picture. Leland Bell's painting in **Fig. A** shows a convincingly three-dimensional figure, made more sculptural by the strong contrasts of light and dark. At the same time the picture is organized with a strong side-to-side movement. The main axis of the figure sweeps horizontally from left to right, rather than from foreground to background. The profile of the furniture is emphasized, adding to the play of

flat, rectangular shapes in the composition, and a flat wall behind the reclining woman further limits the depth.

Systems of perspective for achieving three dimensionality act on the surface in their own special ways. **Fig. B** demonstrates how different vanishing points and eye levels create perspectives which subdivide the total surface into different sized and shaped quadrants. Each rectangle has the same total surface area, but the varied shapes of the triangles result in different kinds of surface composition.

Isometric perspective creates a space that is flatter at the same time that it is deep. In **Fig. C** the subdivisions move evenly across the surface rather than in the centrifugal, focused tunnel of the vanishing point construction.

Over the centuries, artists have invented numberless strategies to link the depth of the page with its surface. Sometimes these linkages can be so elegantly straightforward that we may be unaware of how controlled an apparently casual mark or decision is. In Paul Cézanne's view of Mt. St. Victoire **(Fig. D)**, a generous land-

A

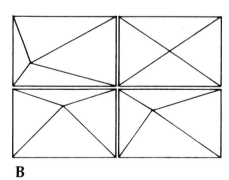

B

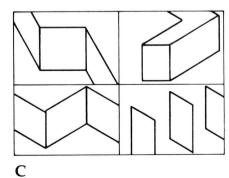

C

scape space is laid out. As the eye moves into the depth of the picture, from the foreground at the bottom edge, across the valley floor that fills the center of the image, to the mountain and finally the distant sky at the top, it runs into a piece of the foreground again, a pine branch overlapping the deepest point in the picture. Cézanne reinforces this link between foreground and background by another means. The up-and-down curve of the mountain range is repeated by the gentle bend of the tree branch. Background (depth) and foreground (flatness) are made to rhyme.

In the Bell, the perspective constructions, and the Cézanne, an effort is made to harmonize the space of two dimensions with that of three dimensions. Sometimes, however, an artist's aim can be to create two- and three-dimensional elements that are clearly separate, that answer one another in a kind of visual counterpoint. The page layout in **Fig. E** is a simple example. Photographs create three-dimensional

windows into the page, which contrast with the flattened right-to-left movements generated by columns of type and headlines. The combination also creates a pattern of lighter and darker shapes across and up and down the page that add up to a dynamic design: a flickering arrangement of solids and voids, contrasting sizes and type weights, combined with an orderly and legible look.

Also see: The Picture Plane, p. 56
         Space Cues: Isometric Perspective, p. 84
         Value Creating Depth, p. 180

Figure A. Leland Bell, ''Ulla at the Cité des Arts (I).'' 1978.

Figure B. Vanishing point perspective.

Figure C. Isometric perspective.

Figure D. Paul Cézanne, ''Mont Sainte-Victoire.'' 1886–1887. (The Phillips Collection, Washington, D.C.)

Figure E. Alina Wheeler and Charles Menasion, Pennsylvania Hospital Annual Report Cover. 1982.

D

E

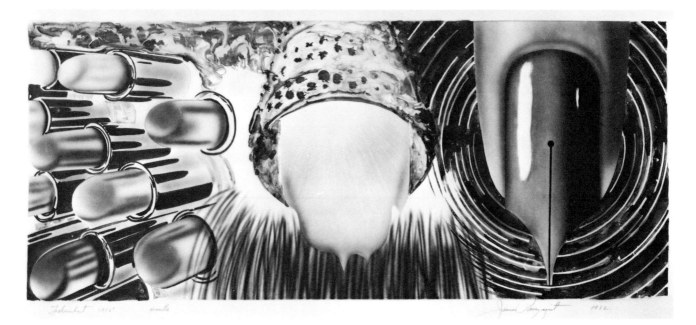

James Rosenquist, ''Fahrenheit 1982 Degrees.'' 1982. (Collection, The Museum of Modern Art, New York; Gift of the Lauder Foundation)

Scale
and
Size

5

Introduction: What Is "Scale"?

A

T HE terms *scale* and *size*, although sometimes used interchangeably, have subtly different meanings. It is important to understand the difference between real size in a work of art and the *feeling* of size that can be conveyed by a page in a book or by a skyscraper.

Real size, large or small, can be impressive. The avalanche of stone represented by the pyramids at Giza (**Fig. A**) is an unforgettable symbol of royal power. When artists have chosen to work at the extremes of size, results have often been startling. A numeral seven feet tall (**Fig. B**) is not just a small thing made bigger: its character is changed. Rather than being just another number, the nine in Fig. B seems more like architecture than print.

The size of a tiny painting by Jean Fouquet (**Fig. C**) is also remarkable. The unending detail, structure within structure, creates a sense of the infinity of creation, of forms more varied than we can imagine revealed as through a microscope, the fascination of a world fit into a tiny space.

Our sense of big and small is often related to our own size. That is, we generally think of those things bigger than we are as being large, those smaller than us as small. Visual habits also influence our perception. We have expectations of the "normal" size range of objects. A seven-foot door seems neither large or small, but a seven-foot number seems huge. If we see a flower twenty inches wide, we may call it enormous, but a car of the same size is obviously tiny.

B

Scale is another matter. Something is said to have a large or small scale not only on the basis of its actual size, but on the feeling of size that it seems to project. A small design may give us an impression of bigness and open space, as does the little painting by Louisa Matthiasdottir (**Fig. D**). At the same time, a large form may have a small scale. A huge skyscraper, like the one in **Fig. E,** may look like a tiny object blown up to a great size, an oversized package of staples, curiously out of scale with its surroundings.

Big scale at a big size is *different* from big scale at a small size. The same is true of small scale. Artists continue to be fascinated by the possibilities and contradictions size and scale can generate.

C

E

D

Figure A. Pyramids of Mycerinus (c. 2500 B.C.), Chephren (c. 2530 B.C.), and Cheops (c. 2570 B.C.), Egypt.

Figure B. Chermayeff and Geismar Associates, ''Nine,'' 57th Street, New York.

Figure C. Jean Fouquet, ''The Taking of Jerico.'' c. 1470. (Bibliothèque Nationale, Paris)

Figure D. Louisa Matthiasdottir, ''2 Sheep, Yellow Sky.'' 1984.

Figure E. World Trade Center towers.

Also see: Visual Biases, p. 234

Scale/Size Relationships

Figure A. A. M. Cassandre, "L'Atlantique." 1931.

Figure B. Giovanni Battista Piranesi, "The Prisons (plate 10)." 1720–1778. (The Metropolitan Museum of Art, New York; Harris Brisbane Dick Fund, 1937)

Figure D. James Rosenquist, "Farenheit 1982 Degrees." 1982. (Collection, The Museum of Modern Art, New York; Gift of the Lauder Foundation)

W<small>E</small> categorize things as "large" or "small" by comparing them with other things. If we say, "That woman is tall," we mean that she is tall compared with most other women. If we say "The Great Pyramid at Giza is huge," we are saying that it is bigger than most other forms in its visual environment; it's quite small compared with a mountain. If we could imagine the pyramid floating alone in an outer space without stars or planets, then it would have no scale; it would seem neither large nor small.

We judge scale in works of art in the same way. A shape, letterform, or color area is seen as part of a web of size comparisons within the work itself. It is important to remember that a work of art establishes its own scale. Whether we are looking at a drawing a few inches high or an image the size of a billboard, it is the size relationships that create the feeling of largeness or smallness.

The contrast between the tiny tugboat and the looming shape that seems to swallow it evokes the huge scale of an ocean liner in A. M. Cassandre's poster in **Fig. A.** We can feel this very clearly despite the size of the reproduction in this book and without knowing the actual dimensions of the poster. Piranesi similarly contrasted the antlike scale of humans with the cavernous spaces of an imagined architecture to create the colossal scale of his prisons in **Fig. B.**

In addition to comparing one form with another in a composition, we can also contrast forms with the size of the overall format. Forms look progressively smaller as the page upon which they sit grows larger **(Fig. C).**

We can see how much we depend on notions of relative size in establishing scale when we look at James Rosenquist's painting in **Fig. D,** in which a shifting scale creates a deliberate confusion about size. Every object is given its own size, independent of its neighbor. "Normal" size is impossible to determine and the usual comparisons between objects are discarded in an explosive and raucous image.

A

B

C

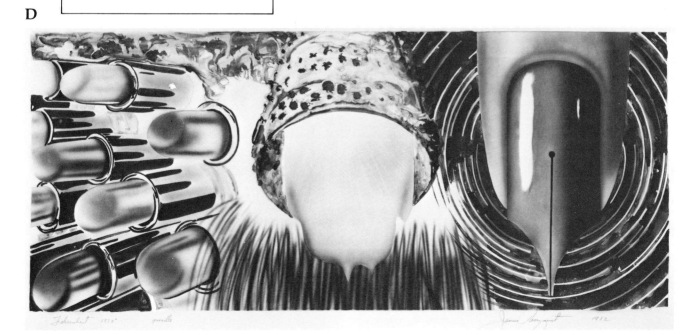

D

Microstructure/Macrostructure

Most forms and images have two aspects: A *microstructure* or small structure, made of details, textures, and small forms fitted together, and a *macrostructure* or large structure, made of large masses that envelop the smaller forms. The sense of scale can be controlled by the emphasis that is given to either one or the other of these structural principles.

The sixteenth-century suit of armor in **Fig. A** articulates both a macro and a microstructure of the human body. Our eyes cannot resist breaking down the mass of the body into smaller components. These units in turn contain still smaller subdivisions, just as the structure of a tree is arranged in levels from trunk to branches to twigs.

It is possible to create an impression of large scale by deemphasizing detail and emphasizing larger, simpler forms. This feeling of grand scale can be accomplished even in a tiny work. Picasso's painting in **Fig. B** is slightly more than 4 by 6 inches, but the harmonious simplification, the editing out of wrinkles, bumps, and folds, the emphasis on big, easily seen forms rather than small ones, gives the impression of a massive and weighty figure.

The tremendous variety and number of visual events, details, large and small shapes, and

A

B

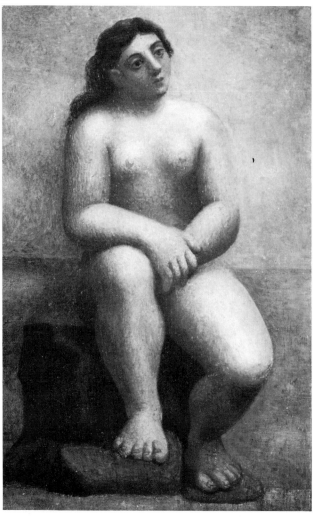

letterforms, create a rich microstructure in Winfred Gaul's poster **(Fig. C).** The eye is invited to inspect closely, linger, and lose itself in the maze of shape and texture that the artist lays out.

Léger, by contrast, organizes his image around a few large and simply drawn areas, giving this poster the quick impact of a brightly colored flag **(Fig. D).**

These examples are simplifications at best. A work that was all macrostructure, all initial impact with nothing for the viewer to discover after the first moment, would be boring indeed, while one that was all microstructure, all detail with no larger organization, would be tedious. Most works of art seek a balance between the big structure which ''grabs'' us, and the smaller forms and relationships which ''keep'' us. The nature of where that proper balance is found depends upon the nature of the artist and the in-

tention of the work. A poster for the subway might want a strong and unified visual impact, whereas a book illustration might reasonably allow the viewer to untangle its structure more slowly.

Also see: Hierarchy/Subdivision, p. 28
Texture, p. 64

Figure A. Suit of Armor for Sir George Clifford. c. 1590. (The Metropolitan Museum of Art, New York; Munsey Fund, 1932)

Figure B. Pablo Picasso, ''Nude Seated on a Rock.'' 1921. (Collection, The Museum of Modern Art, New York; James Thrall Soby Bequest)

Figure C. Winfred Gaul, ''Meditative Images.'' 1960. (Collection, The Museum of Modern Art, New York; Gift of the designer)

Figure D. Fernand Léger, ''F. Léger Museum Marsbroich Leverkusen.'' 1955. (Collection, The Museum of Modern Art, New York; Gift of Mourlot Frères)

C

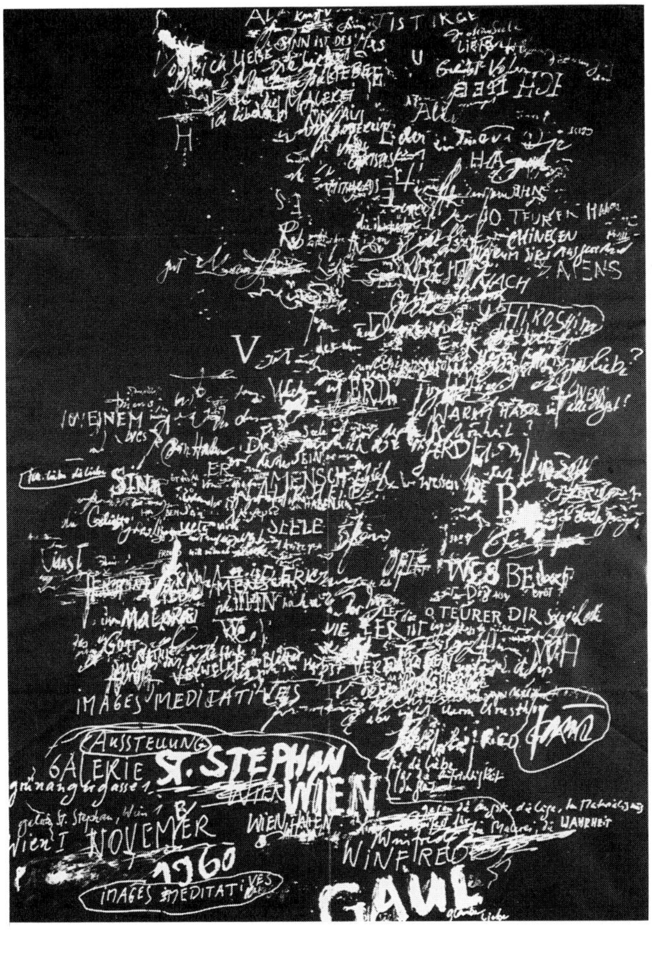

D

Monumental Scale

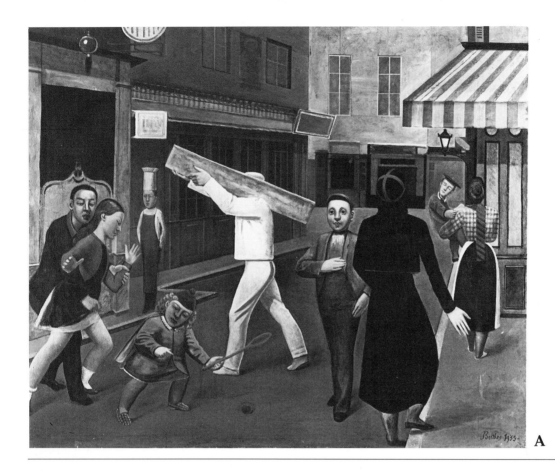

A

I**N** the past, large scale has been used to signify importance and to communicate to large audiences in a large space. For example, imagine an actor on a stage trying to perform a simple action, such as drinking a glass of water. If he does it "naturally," as he might do it offstage, the audience may not be able to see what is happening. In order for the action to be visible over a distance, his gestures must become simpler, bigger, and stripped of small movements. He might exaggerate the tilt of his arm or head, or arch his entire body.

Such large-scale gestures are meant to function in a large space. In the visual arts this kind of scale has often been used to give importance to a subject. A typical example is the simple, forceful pantomime of "The Street," by Balthus **(Fig. A).**

When we describe an image as being monumental in scale, we are referring not to its actual size, but to a feeling it gives of being aggressive, of commanding its environment and extending its authority outward. It seizes our attention and communicates directly and immediately.

The large and simple gesture, with its heroic overtones, can be made in nonrepresentational images as well. The painting by Robert Motherwell **(Fig. B)** is dominated by huge, dark, and easily read shapes which hover like thunderclouds in the composition, barely contained by the edges of the canvas.

Monumental scale can even be felt in so diminutive a form as a single letter of type. The typeface in **Fig. C** is static and massive looking, as dense and weighty as a line of cinderblocks. The casually graceful typeface in **Fig. D,** by comparison, is small in scale, full of delicate and lightweight lines that evoke handwriting.

Interestingly, movies, with their ability to enlarge small details and make them visible to the most distant viewer, will sometimes deemphasize large-scale gesture and focus instead on a close-up of the actor's face. Something as

B

C

D

E

small as a facial tic, normally visible only to one or two nearby observers, becomes a public monument, visible to a crowd.

Advertising also uses oversized images of small objects and gestures, such as billboard-size soda cans or gigantic hands holding cigarettes. For some modern artists, this technique has suggested new ways to approach subject matter.

Monumental scale is no longer restricted to ''important'' or heroic subjects. The small and the ordinary can be made available for a monumental treatment, as in the room-sized mouse of steel and aluminum by the sculptor Claes Oldenberg **(Fig. E).**

Figure A. Balthus, ''The Street.'' 1933. (Collection, The Museum of Modern Art, New York; James Thrall Soby Bequest)

Figure B. Robert Motherwell, ''Elegy to the Spanish Republic, 70.'' 1961. (The Metropolitan Museum of Art, New York; Anonymous gift, 1965)

Figure E. Claes Oldenberg, ''Geometric Mouse—Scale A.'' 1975. (Collection, The Museum of Modern Art, New York; Blanchette Rockefeller Fund)

Also see: Weight of Shape, p. 130

The Signatory Line, p. 138

The Impersonal Line, p. 140

Anti-Monumental Scale/Intimate Scale

Some artists evoke a close-up or private feeling in their work, as opposed to the public manner of monumental art. An image that has intimate scale has a one-to-one relationship with its audience. A work of art may have this feeling regardless of its actual size.

Anti-monumental art may often tend toward the whimsical or casual looking, in contrast to the serious subject matter we generally associate with monumental images. The painter Paul Klee was often fascinated and inspired by tiny things—the pattern of fish scales, forms of seed pods and small plants, tendrils and wiry forms of growing things (Fig. A). The private, hand-held size of these forms, observed as though through a microscope, seems suited to the essentially dreamy, secret, and self-absorbed feeling of a charming puzzle.

When we look at the painting in Fig. B, we are drawn into its mysterious landscape of fragile forms, delicate textures, and jewel-like color. It seems we cannot get close enough to absorb or even to see it all. The delicate filigree of ornament on the page demand a slow, luxurious examination of the forms themselves as well as the meaning of the text.

Book design, by its very nature, lends itself to an anti-monumental approach. A book is viewed closely by a single reader, and reading is basically a private activity requiring focused attention. The designer therefore can work with small and fairly complex forms, certain that the viewer will be able to take it all in. Delicate typefaces, rich ornament, and precise forms can work well at this scale, as they do in William Morris' design for text and decoration in Fig. C.

Also see: Enclosed Space, p. 94
Geometric/Organic Shape, p. 126

Figure A. Paul Klee, ''Around the Fish.'' 1926. (Collection, The Museum of Modern Art, New York; Abby Aldrich Rockefeller Fund)

Figure B. Darbár of Jahāngīr, from a Jahāngīr-nāma manuscript. Mughal School, c. 1620. (Courtesy, Museum of Fine Arts, Boston; Francis Bartlett Donation of 1912 and Picture Fund, 14.654)

Figure C. William Morris, ''Tale of Beowulf.'' 1895. (The Pierpont Morgan Library, New York)

A

B

C

Kasimir Malevich, ''Suprematist Composition with
Trapezium and Square.'' After 1915. (Stedelijk Museum, Amsterdam)

Shape

6

Introduction

SHAPE making is an easily available tool which offers a tremendous power to communicate. Shapes have instantly recognizable visual personalities. We recognize the soft and yielding form of an S curve before we notice that it belongs to a swan's neck or a model posed in a drawing class. Shape, made of cut paper or paint, can also exist independent of any object. Every shape has its own structure of internal forces, thrusts, bulges, centers, and countermovements that create its particular look and power.

In this sense, we can describe shape as a universally understood language. As a trademark, a shape may be used to communicate the identity of a corporation. In a print or painting, a shape may evoke a sense of dread or the power of growing things. As a symbol, a shape may give visible form to an action such as running or jumping. In most cases, it is the shape itself, more than the object depicted, that communicates the idea.

Shape is a visible record of the way we organize forces on the flat surface.

Figure A. Sengai Gibon, ''Circle, Triangle, Square.'' c. 1800. (Idemitsu Museum of Arts, Tokyo)

A

How Are Shapes Generated?

Wᴇ generally think of a shape as being defined by a clear edge, but we can also see shape where there is no edge at all. In **Fig. A** we see a shape without a clear border. The small dashes form a pattern of visual forces which group and compress to form a triangle. Shape is generated not by outline, but rather by a *structural skeleton*, a pattern made by the main structural landmarks. In this case we recognize triangularity as thrusting out in three directions. By adjusting or changing the degree of that thrust in any direction, we could get a number of different triangles. The outline is the *result* rather than the cause of these different patterns of force. In **Fig. B** we sense the structural skeletons themselves creating shape. Whenever we see shape, whether in a diagram like this one or in a complicated work of art, we are always aware of this tension between an inner structure and a skin or outline stretched over that skeleton. When the skin seems to be pulled tautly around a stiff skeleton, as it does in geometric shapes, we perceive those shapes as "hard." When the skin seems instead to bulge and bag over an indeterminate skeleton, as in the saggy shape of an amoeba, the shape seems soft and relaxed. That is why a shape can feel "soft" despite a crisp, sharply drawn edge, or "hard" even when an outline is not easily perceived.

We are able to see a clear shape, another triangle, in the complicated group in **Fig. C.** Here we see the same configuration of forces as in the Fig. B triangle, a stable and broad base with a focal point at the top of the mass.

Our perceptual mechanism, our eye and brain together, wants to organize the information it receives, to see the large patterns of force influencing the scattered parts. Just as we instantly perceive triangularity in the complicated outline of a group of figures, we also will perceive shape when offered only a minimal amount of visual information. *Closure* is this tendency for our eyes to fill in the gaps, to string together separate shapes or lines and see a larger structural pattern, completing an incomplete pattern with our eyes.

Fig. D demonstrates how the principle of closure can generate shape. We cannot resist

seeing shapes here, although no explicit line defines a complete contour. The same thing happens when we look at the drawing by Fairfield Porter in **Fig. E.** Here the image of a landscape is broken into six roughly rectangular patches. The divisions are strong enough, that is, each rectangle is far enough away from its neighbor, so that we almost see a page with six separate views. The overall image, on the verge of break-

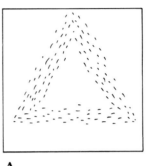

A

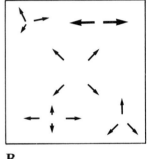

B

C

ing into smaller pieces, knits itself back together again as we read the long vertical movements of the tree trunks.

In the poster by Leo Lionni (Fig. F) clearly defined shapes join in this same way to form a larger, more complex shape. Five simple and clear individual shapes are placed on a surface, and seen together they add up to a seated figure with a typewriter. We are able simultaneously to see this image and to enjoy the lively and eccentric thrusts, tensions, and particularities of each of the five original shapes.

Also see: Gestalt, p. 6
Grouping, p. 60
Implied Line, p. 144

Figure C. Raphael, ''St. George and the Dragon.'' 1505–1506. (National Gallery of Art, Washington; Hellon Collection)

Figure E. Fairfield Porter, ''Study.'' (Collection of Whitney Museum of American Art; Gift of Alex Katz; Acq. #77.63)

Figure F. Leo Lionni, ''Olivetti Lettera 22.'' 1956. (Collection, The Museum of Modern Art, New York; Gift of the Olivetti Corporation)

D

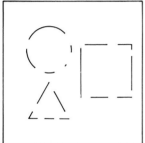

E

F

Simple/Complex Shape

SIMPLE shapes are shapes that have a structure easily grasped by the eye. One way to test a shape for simplicity is to try to draw it from memory. The simple shape will have a clear order to its parts, angles, and directions that can be remembered at a glance. Simple shapes have an emblematic character, an easy-to-see quality and a forcefulness. Geometric shapes tend to be relatively simple in this way.

Complex shapes, in contrast, do not reveal their structures to the eye as readily. They invite the eye to linger and explore, to analyze and understand more slowly. They offer a different kind of visual richness.

We can see this difference if we compare the two fairly straightforward shapes in **Fig. A.** Each has the same number of parts, sides, and angles, yet the one on the left is regular and graspable with equal angles, lengths of side, and parallel directions, while the one on the right clearly has a more varied interaction of forces.

A simple shape may have many parts, but if they are arranged on a simple structural skeleton, the impact of a simple visual statement will be preserved.

A designer faced with working out a system of signs meant to communicate to people in a hurry who may not speak the same language might favor clear and simple shape for its ability to communicate directly and quickly. **Fig. B** distills a characteristic shape from the typical gesture or pose of a number of different activities in a memorable way.

Simple shape becomes a blunt and forceful statement in Richard Serra's lithograph in **Fig. C.** Rather than inventing a complex and many-featured composition, Serra's print has a literal and all-at-once impact.

A page from a medieval manuscript is intended to stand up to a long look **(Fig. D).** Even to a modern viewer, accustomed to the parade of colors and shapes found in any weekly magazine, the richness of this design comes across. To a twelfth-century person, unused to a wide range of artificial color and complex shape, such a page must have been an endless feast of intense visual experiences.

Complex shape is generally more dynamic than simple shape. Since a shape is a container full of two-dimensional movements, more complicated shapes contain a more complicated structure of internal thrusts. This is, at least in part, the challenge and interest the figure has held for artists for so many centuries, an endlessly complex container of numberless forces, yet one that can be described in the language of complexity **(Fig. E)** or in the more cerebral one of simple shape **(Fig. F).**

Also see: Anti-Monumental Scale, p. 114
Visual Information, p. 236

Figure B. Yoshiro Yamashita, designer, Pictographs for Sigvage at the Tokyo Olympic Games. 1964.

Figure C. Richard Serra, ''Untitled.'' 1972. (Collection of Whitney Museum of American Art; Gift of Susan Morse Hilles; Acq. #74.10)

Figure D. Incarnation initial from the ''Book of Kells.'' Early 9th century. (The Board of Trinity College, Dublin)

Figure E. James Valerio, ''Tightrope Walker.'' 1981. (Private collection)

Figure F. Alexander Archipenko, ''Woman with Fan.'' 1915. (Hirshhorn Museum and Sculpture Garden, Smithsonian Institution; Gift of Joseph H. Hirshhorn, 1966)

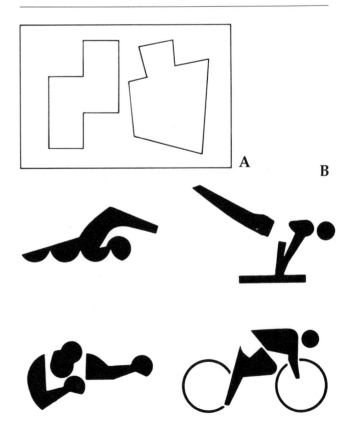

A   B

C

D

E

F

Positive/Negative Shape

WHEN a single shape is put onto a flat field, as in **Fig. A,** at least two shapes are created. The figure shape, the one placed on the field, is often called a *positive* shape, and the shapes formed by the "uncovered" parts of the field are called *negative* shapes. Positive and negative shape is really an aspect of the figure/ground relationship which we have already looked at.

Most people tend to notice only the shapes of objects and are less conscious of the shapes of intervals between the objects. Obviously, each of these shapes depends on the other. If the angle of the legs of a human figure change, so will the space in between. If we draw one kind of shape, we are drawing the other kind at the same time. Many artists have trouble seeing a shape because they are focused on the positive shape but not considering the negative. When we design negative shapes, we give form to emptiness.

An illustration from Albrecht Dürer's book on the proper formation of letters gives us a glimpse of the thinking involved in shaping a letterform. Dürer seems to treat the letter as the negative space. Measurements, subdivisions, and curves are plotted in the space around the letter, and in the resulting letter the negative shapes are as carefully made as the positive ones **(Fig. B).**

When negative space competes for our attention rather than remaining subordinate to positive shape, we often get double readings. Pentagram's design for a logo for London's National Theatre **(Fig. C)** is a witty use of this now-you-see-it-now-you-don't effect. It creates a shape which appears to be constantly in motion, not only on its fluid and changing outside edge, but in the flickering back and forth between one reading and another.

We have already seen how convexity and concavity affect our reading of the figure/ground relationship. The swelling outward of a shape tends to create figure (positive shape), while shapes whose boundaries curve inward are read as ground (negative shapes). Concave and convex shapes also create particular kinds of visual space.

A drawing made with the kind of bulging outline seen in **Fig. D** shows us form expanding, actively pressing against the surrounding emptiness. Here, positive shape, the powerful look of a solid volume, a swollen sack of forms covered with a single skin, triumphs over negative shape.

The relationship is reversed in the Giacometti drawing in **Fig. E.** Here the surrounding space is not passive and empty but invades the shape of the figure, scooping chunks out of the positive space. When the artist treats surrounding space as an extremely active element, the positive form may be reduced to a skeletal frame for negative space. In the Giacometti, for example, the form of the figure is scarred and eaten into by the surrounding space until it becomes a sliver of form surrounded by immensity.

Also see: Figure/Ground, p. 70
Figure/Ground Strategies, p. 72
The Shifting Edge, p. 148

Figure B. Albrecht Dürer, "Construction of the letter G." c. 1525.

Figure C. Pentagram Design, "National Theatre Logo." (Pentagram Ltd., London)

Figure D. Gaston Lachaise, "Nude." c. 1930. (The Metropolitan Museum of Art, New York; Gift of George T. Delacorte, Jr., 1957)

Figure E. Alberto Giacometti, "Grand Figure (Tall Figure)." 1947. (Collection, Pierre Matisse Gallery, New York)

A

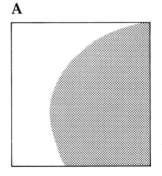

B

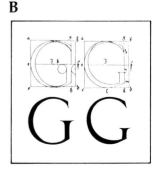

Geometric/Organic Shape

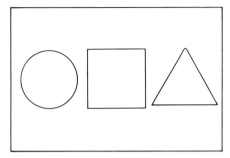

A   D

Geometry is a branch of mathematics that deals with measurements, quantities, and relationships by turning them into points, lines, planes, and shapes. It is different from other branches of math that deal with the same things by turning them into numbers and symbols. Geometry is numbers given a physical form, made visible.

All geometric shapes seem to have been made by some process of the intellect as well as by the hand. The straight edge, the regular and smooth curve, and the sharp angle are all aspects of geometric shape. The most common of the many geometric constructions are the circle, the square, and the triangle **(Fig. A)**.

Geometric shape looks absolute, uncontaminated by accidents, outside of any style, and universally understandable. Even geometric shape that is found in nature—in seedpods, seashells, mineral crystals—has a timeless look, giving an impression of creation rather than growth **(Fig. B)**.

Even with its out-of-this-world perfection, however, geometry can seem alive and immediate. This was one of the reasons that it appealed to so many early modernist artists seeking a universal visual language. In **Fig. C** we can see the legible, clean, harmonious, finished look of geometry. However, the composition appears lively, partly because, while the forms seem to be rationally engineered with ruler and compass, their placement in the rectangle seems to be the result of intuitive choice on the part of the artist.

The legibility and clarity of geometry makes it appealing to designers whose work often combines geometric letterforms with uncluttered organization of information. Paul Renner's poster in **Fig. D** is a good example of early modern design meant to be visible within the noisy distractions of a modern city. The variety of rectangles echo the rectangle of the poster itself, and contrasts, such as the large curves of the *B* against the straight lines of the composition, stand out with the brightness and impact of a traffic signal.

Geometry by itself, of course, is not a magic key to good design. The final responsibility for

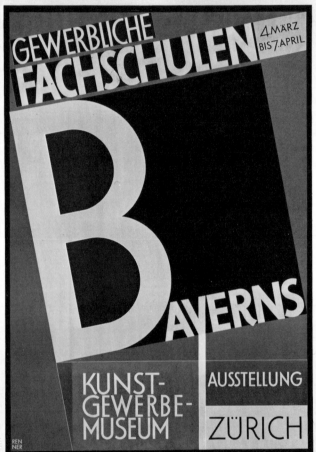

Figure C. Kasimir Malevich, ''Suprematist Composition with Trapezium and Square.'' After 1915. (Stedelijk Museum, Amsterdam)

Figure D. Paul Renner, ''Fachschulen Bayerns.'' 1928. (Kunstgewerbemuseum de Stadt, Zurich)

making instinctive or intuitive decisions about shape or placement remains with the artist, and the test of a work of art is not whether it is made correctly according to a set of rules, but whether it *looks* right. If it *looks* right, it *is* right.

C

Organic shapes are shapes that have neither straight edges nor regular curves. When we speak of ''natural'' forms and shapes, we are usually referring to organic shape. We can see that the natural geometric structures in Fig. B seem mechanical and not nearly as lively as the more organic looking ones in **Fig. E.**

Organic shapes look grown rather than made, and we apply the term *biomorphic* (meaning having a shape that lives) to shapes of this kind. The gradually changing profile of a bone, for instance, shows us how the shape ex-

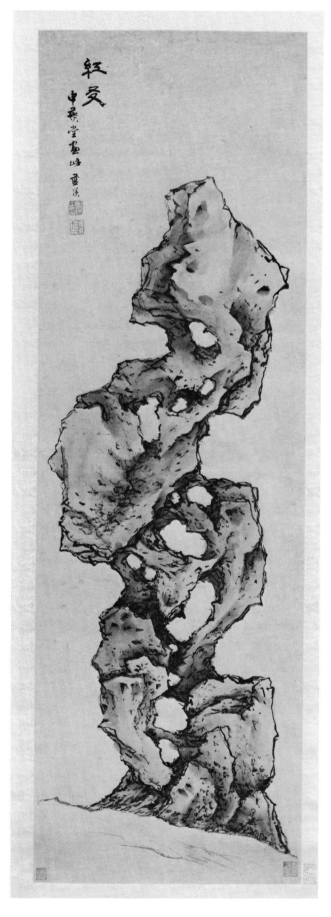

紅友
申樂堂畫此藍瑛

F

panded, contracted, and changed during its process of development. This feeling that the shape is inhabited by living forces is what makes organic shape interesting.

The decorative and fantastically shaped rock in **Fig. F,** part of a Chinese ornamental garden, is a type of form prized in Chinese art for its unimaginably complicated shape. Pockmarked and hollowed out by endless bites of empty space, it presents a whole new and unexpected profile and set of internal shapes to the eye with every change in the viewer's position.

Organic shape, especially plant and flower forms, formed the basic vocabulary of the Art Nouveau movement in the early twentieth century. The composition in **Fig. G** is overgrown with stems, tendrils, and curvilinear rhythms which together make an almost unbearably lively surface. The perfected feeling of geometric shape and the lively energy of organic form can be made to blend, contrast, and reinforce one another, however. The beautiful brush drawing in **Fig. H** is a surprising example of this combination. Geometric form treated in the organic and calligraphic style of Chinese art yields an image that is both casual and perfect.

Also see: Straightness, p. 36

Monumental Scale, p. 112

Anti-Monumental Scale, p. 114

Materials & Line Qualities, p. 142

Figure F. Lan Ying, ''Red Friend.'' (The Metropolitan Museum of Art; Gift of Mr. and Mrs. Earl Morse, in honor of Douglas Dillon, 1979)

Figure G. Jan Toorop, Poster for ''Delftsche Slaolie.'' 1894. (Courtesy of the Library of Congress)

Figure H. Sengai Gibon, ''Circle, Triangle, Square.'' c. 1800. (Idemitsu Museum of Arts, Tokyo)

G

H

Weight of Shape

THE weight of a shape is, of course, a visual weight. Its heaviness or lightness is measured by the eye. There are some simple principles through which artists can control visual weight. Regular and geometric shapes tend to look heavier than irregular shapes; the circle, square, and triangle in **Fig. A** are visually weightier than the organic forms in the same figure. Similarly, a symmetrical shape, geometric or otherwise, will seem heavier than an asymmetrical one **(Fig. B)**.

Compare the weight of Kurt Schwitters' collage composition in **Fig. C** with the bouyant feeling of Kandinsky's shapes in **Fig. D.** At the same time, notice that the tiny geometric forms in the Kandinsky create strong accents, points of weight and stability in a composition filled with movement.

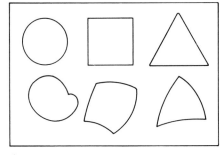

A

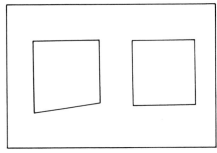

B

C

A weight of a shape will also be affected by its position in the composition. A shape placed in the center of a field or in the upper part of a composition will seem heavier than the same shape off-center or lower down **(Fig. E).**

Texture and value also affect visual weight. Compare the shapes in **Fig. F.** As texture and/ or light to dark values move across the shape, we notice an increase in the sense of density and in the feeling of sculptural three dimensionality.

Also see: Balance, p. 18
Top & Bottom, p. 48
Left & Right, p. 50
Weight of Value, p. 174
Weight of Color, p. 212

Figure C. Kurt Schwitters, ''Merz Drawing.'' 1924. (Collection, The Museum of Modern Art, New York; Katherine S. Dreier Bequest)

Figure D. Wassily Kandinsky, ''Isolated Objects.'' 1934. (Philadelphia Museum of Art; The Louise and Walter Arensberg Collection)

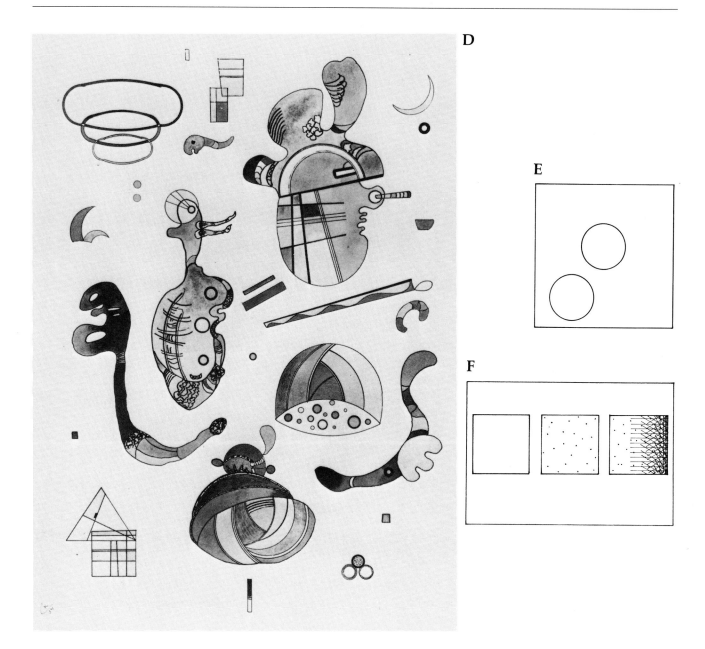

D

E

F

Tension & Shape

THE circle, square, and triangle have an unchanging or irreducible look. We can see other shapes as combinations of these forms. For instance, a rectangle might be constructed of squares, or a shape may be made from a circle and triangle **(Fig. A)**. The three "basic" shapes, however, like the three primary colors, are not made of anything but themselves. They have a completeness and a purity that make them visually restful.

Still, it would be a dull world to look at if everything conformed to one of these three shapes. As a welcome change from simple geometric shape, we appreciate some visual excitement and tension in art as we do elsewhere. We can effect this visual tension by taking a simple or regular shape and deforming it.

The sense of tension is similar to what we feel when we stretch a rubber band and feel it trying to return to its unstretched state. Similarly, an oval is a circle "stretched" in one direction; the second shape in **Fig. B** is a square stretched and compressed at the same time. In each case we perceive a force which seems to push a regular form out of shape. The more visual forces at work in a design, the more tension is increased.

A simple but effective vocabulary of tension in deformation can be seen in the shapes in **Fig. C**. We can sense the "normal" shape of each figure, and visual tension is the result of a perceived gap between that norm image and its deformation.

In the painting by El Greco **(Fig. D)** a deformation of shape is also visible, a stretching out of the proportions of each figure as if some tremendous vertical force were pulling the figures upward. This force also extends through such details as drapery. This highly expressive distortion of shape is often found in the work of Expressionist artists, from El Greco to Van Gogh.

Another way of increasing the sense of tension in a shape is by changing its orientation, its position in relation to the vertical and horizontal. The square in **Fig. E,** resting solidly on its bottom edge, conveys an almost immovable stability. The same shape, placed so that its edges form diagonals, has a different look altogether. It now stands on point, performing a balancing act that is a tension-filled visual event. The balance is precarious—it could collapse at any moment—and the once stable square is now a diamond, filled with the potential for motion and change.

Also see: Harmony/Dissonance, p. 16
Tension, p. 20
Proportional Systems, p. 38
Directed Tension, p. 156

Figure C. Geometric forms based on shapes by Ivan Klium, c. 1917.

Figure D. El Greco, "Madonna and Child with Saint Martina and Saint Agnes." 1597–1599. (National Gallery of Art, Washington; Widener Collection)

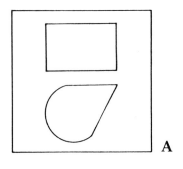

A

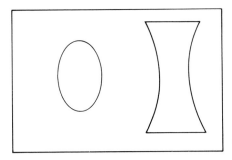

B

C

D

E

Pablo Picasso, ''Sculptor at Rest Before a Small Torso.'' 1933.
(Collection, The Museum of Modern Art, New York; Purchase
Fund)

Line

Introduction: Line Qualities

THE line—long, thin, straight, curvy—is in many ways the most useful of all the graphic tools.

Even as children we understood the delights of drawing lines. With them we could create a frozen record of our arm's path across the page. This line, sometimes smooth and rhythmic, sometimes rapidly changing direction, expressed body movement in a two-dimensional language. One line crossing over another created an illusion of space and volume, one part of the line seeming to lie in front of another. Also, by making a line connect back with itself, like the snake biting its tail, we could create closed shapes; organizing the surface and controlling the tangle of lines by "outlining," isolating one part from the rest.

These needs to express hand and arm gestures in two dimensions and to define, organize, and contain are basic to all artists.

Line can capture and make sensible a lot of visual information in a rapid and simple way. It has marvelous range and variety—intimate, direct, expressive. Drawing, which frequently relies on line, is the basic visualizing tool for most two- and three-dimensional art and design, from the simplest to the most complex.

The cliché, "there are no lines in nature," also points to a special quality of line. More than color or value or texture, line is an abstraction, an invention that allows us to mediate between the object or space that we see and its two-dimensional equivalent drawn or printed on a page. We do not necessarily have to depend on seeing a linear element in nature in order to find a use for line in a drawing or design. Many non-linear qualities can be expressed using line.

The agile and responsive line in the drawing by Rembrandt in **Fig. A** does much more than simply outline objects or repeat lines seen on the model. Here line sketches out the big rhythms of the composition and the changes in texture and light. It gives us an almost transparent sense of the armature or skeleton inside a form, and it can catch the most elusive and fleeting gestures and effects. The line also animates the drawing, filling it with visual movement.

Beyond this, the line maps out a pattern of forces active in the space. The thrust and counterthrust of shapes, the interpenetration of lights and darks, the shifting feeling of space as we move through it, can all be expressed through line.

Figure A. Rembrandt van Rijn, "Beheading of Prisoners." (The Metropolitan Museum of Art, New York; Robert Lehman Collection, 1975)

A

The Signatory Line

A pen, brush, or pencil moving over a flat surface can become a sort of seismograph, a delicate and precise instrument for recording the tiniest motion or change of pressure of the hand holding the drawing tool. More pressure can result in a heavier, darker, crisper line, less pressure in a lighter, softer, less uniform line. As a line changes from thin to thick, it seems to be inhabited by forces, reflecting the life of the hand.

The artist chooses how much control to exert over the movement of the hand. **Fig. A** illustrates that a word can be written in a carefully controlled way, in which attention is paid to proper letter formation, or can be written in a more hurried way. As we write more quickly, the natural flow of the hand takes over and influences (or even destroys) the appearance of the letters. Legibility is exchanged for an expressive, lively line. The artist determines where to strike the balance between legibility (clarity) and the signature, gestural quality of the hand.

Fig. B, a drawing by Lennart Anderson, is a study in control. The line follows the form of the model as closely as possible, and one senses that the changes in its weight and direction are the direct result of the artist's carefully observing the form itself. The action of the hand is subordinated to the description of the form of the figure.

In the drawing by Tintoretto **(Fig. C)** the motion of the hand becomes more noticeable and insistent. A series of short, broken curves and dashes, varying from light and ghostly looking to heavy and muscular, make a sturdily built, dynamic figure. The line is constantly moving in different directions.

Finally, in the drawing by Willem De Kooning **(Fig. D)** the form of the figure is obliterated by emphasis on the handwriting quality of the line. The personal "handwriting" character of line, which we first noticed as children, stays visible in the work of mature artists. The handwriting of each of these three drawings is entirely different, as unique as a fingerprint or a voice pattern.

The handmade quality of a signature line often creates a sense of intimacy, a familiar human mark with which the viewer can empathize. Joseph and Melissa Gilbert's poster **(Fig. E)** magnifies and focuses on this quality. Variations in heaviness, direction, and shape make a casual and graceful typographic image which contrasts with the stable presence of the text in the lower right. An artist may also be aided by a choice of tools that are well suited to picking up the smallest twitch of the hand, in this case a brush dipped in thin, flowing ink.

SIGNATURE
SIGNATURE
SIGNATURE

A   B

C

D

E

Figure B. Lennart Anderson, ''Male Figure Study for Idylls I and III.'' 1977.

Figure C. Jacopo Tintoretto, ''Standing Youth with His Arm Raised.'' (National Gallery of Art, Washington; Ailsa Mellon Bruce Fund)

Figure D. Willem DeKooning, ''(Untitled) (Woman).'' 1961. (Hirshhorn Museum and Sculpture Garden, Smithsonian Institution; Gift of Joseph H. Hirshhorn, 1966)

Figure E. Joseph and Melissa Gilbert, ''Bell Gallery, Brown University.'' 1982.

Also see: Mark Making, p. 62

Anti-Monumental Scale, p. 114

Pictorial/Actual Motion, p. 154

The Impersonal Line

Calder 1932 **A**

SOMETIMES artists deemphasize the personal and expressive qualities of a line, such as varying weight and direction, in order to create a more depersonalized or purified line.

The drawing by Alexander Calder in **Fig. A** is built from a wavering, wandering line which gives the impression of a hand in casual control of itself. The irregularities of curvature and direction are obviously "handmade," but the heaviness of the line is as mechanical and unchanging as a metal wire. Calder did, in fact, use wire to construct three-dimensional forms, and this mechanical aspect of the line is a witty visual comment about the similarities between his wire sculpture and his drawing. It's also a comical image of modern times: an impersonal line used to make a personal and whimsical picture.

The Naum Gabo sculpture in **Fig. B** is also made with a line of uniform weight, but another aspect of "handwriting" is supressed. Variations in direction are limited. Curves are more regular, as if drawn with a compass. The line is more reserved looking. Whereas Calder's figures seem to be made from a continuous strand of wire unrolled from a spool, these lines seem like separate segments fitted together to form an architectural unit. The more formal approach

Figure A. Alexander Calder, "Cowboys Roping a Steer." 1932. (Philadelphia Museum of Art; Purchased, Lola Downin Peck Fund, From Carl and Laura Zigrosser Collection)

Figure B. Naum Gabo, "Translucent Variations on Spheric Themes." 1951. (Solomon R. Guggenheim Museum, New York)

Figure C. Al Held, "Volta V." 1977. (Hirshhorn Museum and Sculpture Garden, Smithsonian Institution; Museum Purchase, 1978)

"cools down" the sensual curviness of the volume.

The painting by Al Held **(Fig. C)** still further minimizes any sign of the gesture of the hand. There are differences in line weight, but the thickness and thinness are not products of the hand's pressure at all. The line weights here are all intellectual choices, executed with masking tape. In addition, any irregular wandering of the line is eliminated by the use of ruler and compass. The result is an image of powerful clarity and control; the imprint of the body is replaced by impersonal, self-contained forces which move through the canvas without noticing one another.

Also see: Mark Making, p. 62
Monumental Scale, p. 112

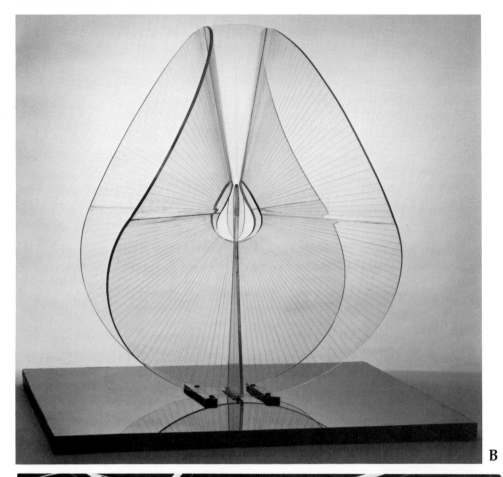

B

C

Materials & Line Qualities

THE quality or "look" of a line can be affected by the material (or medium) used to make the line and by the method or tool used to apply the line to the surface.

Materials have ranged from thin and flowing media like ink or paint, to heavier bodied charcoal or pastel sticks, hard and soft pencils and crayons, dry pigments, soot, or powdered earth, and more recently even laser beams. Tools have included brushes of many kinds, pointed nibs of metal or bamboo, fingers dipped in powdered or liquid color, mechanical devices, and even computer printers. All these have been applied to everything from pieces of paper to the surface of the Earth. Each of these media has its own special characteristics or look, and each reacts in its own way to the various tools and application methods **(Fig. A)**.

All materials can be handled in different ways but some are more capable of changing their look than others. Ink, for example, can be as black as a crow's wing or, mixed with water, can make hundreds of lighter tones; it can be hard and precisely linear in a pen as in the drawing by David Hockney in **Fig. B,** or it can be soft edged and blurry when applied with a brush, as in the Dutch drawing in **Fig. C.**

Sometimes the inherent qualities of the material strongly affect the way a work of art evolves. Different materials will resist or aid the artist's attempts to use them in different ways. For example, charcoal smudges easily and can be "worked" from dark to light, from hard to soft edged, from line to tone. It is highly flexible, and skillful artists can make it look very different indeed. The drawing by Degas **(Fig. D)** and the drawing by Henri Matisse **(Fig. E)** are both charcoal on paper. The characteristic charcoal look is recognizable in both, but each artist has chosen his own way of making a line.

Imagine having to work in mosaic, a medium that cannot be smudged, blended, or made thick and thin. Imagine drawing a line with roofing tar, or with enamel paint thrown off the end of a stick. How much would you be able to control the line, and how much would the medium or tool influence the look of the finished piece?

Also see: Mark Making, p. 62

Texture, p. 64

Figure B. David Hockney, "Sir John Gielgud." 1977. (M. H. DeYoung Memorial Museum, The Fine Arts Museums of San Francisco)

Figure C. Nicholas Maes, "The Young Mother." (The Metropolitan Museum of Art, New York; Rogers Fund, 1947)

Figure D. Edgar Degas, "The Violinist," c. 1879. (Courtesy, Museum of Fine Arts, Boston; William Francis Warden Fund; 58.1263)

Figure E. Henri Matisse, "Reclining Nude." 1939. (Collection, The Museum of Modern Art, New York; Purchase.)

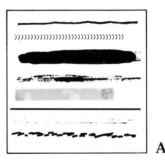

A

B

C

D

E

Implied Line

In describing shape, we discussed lines of force, "invisible lines" that are not drawn but can make themselves felt in any composition. Similar shapes close together are perceived as a group and generate a visual tension. There is a sense of closing the gap between them to create an implied line. **Fig. A** works with this kind of line. Like vertabrae in a spine, the letterforms are linked along a visual path that weaves up and down from left to right.

Rembrandt's "Night Watch" **(Fig. B)** creates a similar kind of visual event. Here, as we move from left to right, the heads form an up-and-down sequence, a complicated rhythmic line like music notes arranged on a stave.

A slightly different type of line occurs in Caravaggio's "Martyrdom of St. Matthew" **(Fig. C).** Here the direction in which each person is looking forms a criss-crossing web of forces, implied lines which cross like swords in a tense composition.

Another kind of implied line is a structural axis, such as the twisting line that we perceive running through a spiral staircase. The small sculpture by Henri Matisse in **Fig. D** has this kind of structural line at its center. Remember that there is no physical line that we can *see*. We do, however, perceive a linear force that seems to govern the entire mass of the sculpture. What we see is often different from what we perceive.

Also see: Gestalt, p. 6
Rhythm, p. 32
Grouping, p. 60
Directed Tension, p. 156

Figure A. Russell Tatro, "Invitation," for Information Science Incorporated.

Figure B. Rembrandt van Rijn, "Night Watch." 1642. (Rijksmuseum, Amsterdam)

Figure C. Michelangelo Caravaggio, "Martyrdom of St. Matthew." c. 1592–1595. (Church of S. Luigi dei Francesi, Rome)

Figure D. Henri Matisse, "Madeleine I." 1901. (Baltimore Museum of Art; The Cone Collection, formed by Dr. Claribel Cone and Miss Etta Cone of Baltimore, Md.)

A

B

C

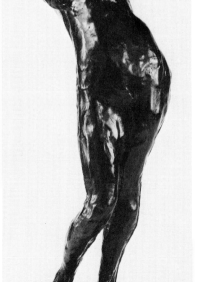

D

The Line as Edge: The Contour Line

Outlines that travel around the silhouette of a form also influence the inside area they enclose. The contour of any shape, simple or complicated, forms a kind of container for the two-dimensional forces, the internal pushes and pulls that seem to make the shape bulge out or press inward **(Fig. A)**.

Even a quickly made contour drawing can convey a certain amount of information about a form. When the single contour line encloses a very large area, however, it tends to appear flat, like a string lying on the page, and thus loses its ability to describe three-dimensional space. When an artist wishes to emphasize flatness rather than space, the single contour is very useful. In **Fig. B,** for example, the line does not so much dig into the space but rather forms a beautiful two-dimensional rhythm across the page.

The woodcut by Felix Vallotton in **Fig. C** also uses the large contour to create a field of gently mobile silhouettes. Visual movement takes place at the edge, which we follow like a path, and a strong sense of flat surface counterpoints the generous, deep space in a room full of people.

When contour lines outline smaller areas, or when large areas contain smaller zones, a more solid and three-dimensional form occurs. Picasso uses the contour to describe the edges of the smaller forms inside the large silhouette in his drawing **(Fig. D).** As a result he describes a more complete and clearer three-dimensional form, creating a sculptural solidity even while the line remains light and graceful.

Also see: Figure/Ground, p. 70

Figure/Ground Strategies, p. 72

Color Interpenetration/Changes at the Edge, p. 210

Figure B. Lowell Williams and Lana Rigsby, ''Madrigal and Chamber Choir Festival.''

Figure C. Felix Vallotton, ''La Modiste.''

Figure D. Pablo Picasso, ''Man Seated at a Table.'' 1914. (Collection, The Museum of Modern Art, New York; The John S. Newberry Collection)

A

B

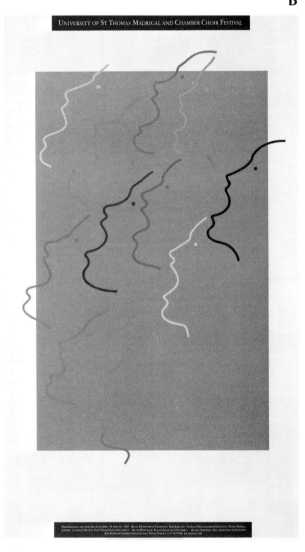

UNIVERSITY OF ST. THOMAS MADRIGAL AND CHAMBER CHOIR FESTIVAL

C

LA MODISTE.   FV

D

The Line as Edge: The Shifting Edge

A common function of the line is to serve as an edge, marking a boundary between one area and another. The line in the print by Picasso in **Fig. A** maps out a network of clear boundaries between the object or figure and its surrounding space. Each area is self-contained and clearly distinct from its neighbors. The line marks a single and definite step from one shape or space to another.

Cézanne thinks of outline in a different way, which can be seen in **Fig. B**. Multiple lines rather than single lines are used to mark the edge of a form and to separate one shape from another. Instead of a one-step boundary between the figure and the surrounding space, a series of steps lead the eye from one shape to another. The multiple lines are a zone of transition in which, for a moment, two spaces flow together. There is no single line at which the surrounding space ends and the figure begins. The line is used here to express the vision of constantly shifting edges which we see as we change our viewing point to scan the surrounding environment.

A

In the drawing by Alberto Giacometti **(Fig. C)** many more steps are added. Although lines tend to pile up along the boundaries between one space and another, they also fill the interior spaces, shuffling the eye constantly through objects and spaces and out again.

B

Figure A. Pablo Picasso, ''Sculptor at Rest Before a Small Torso.'' 1933. (Collection, The Museum of Modern Art, New York; Purchase Fund)

Figure B. Paul Cézanne, ''Seated Nude.'' (Kupferstich-kabinett, Basel)

Figure C. Alberto Giacometti, ''Portrait in an Interior.'' 1951. (Collection, The Museum of Modern Art, New York; Gift of Mr. and Mrs. Eugene Victor Thaw)

Also see: How Are Shapes Generated? p. 120

Stroboscopic Motion, p. 162

Color Interpenetration/Changes at the Edge, p. 210

C

A

B

Line & Three-Dimensional Space

LINE can be a tool for creating the illusion of three-dimensional space.

The drawing by Philip Pearlstein in **Fig. A** uses a series of dotted lines to assist the eye in moving over and across the hills and valleys of the figure's form, as well as to define its silhouette. Pearlstein's line also marks off the places where the surface changes its direction, where two planes come together.

Diagonal lines play a special role in making space on a flat surface. As the edges of diagonal planes, they are often perceived as three-dimensional, moving at an angle to the surface into and out of the picture space, whereas vertical and horizontal lines and planes are read as going up and down, back and forth, across the surface. The print by Hokusai in **Fig. B** relies on our reading of the diagonal as stepping back into the space of the picture.

When a sculptor carves a piece of stone or wood, the chisel leaves cutmarks across the surface of the material. These lines show us how the chisel moved through real space and around the form. When the lines are deliberately left on the sculpture, the direction of every facet of the surface is amplified and easier to see. In the African mask in **Fig. C** such lines repeat the direction of each surface many times, making the mask's movement through space more powerful.

Albrecht Dürer uses a more refined version of the line across the plane in his drawings. In **Fig. D** the cross-hatched lines make us aware of the form inside the silhouette. Instead of just a contour containing an ''empty'' shape, a net of lines is stretched over the surface of the form, and these lines make visible the smallest swellings of a facial muscle or tendon.

Also see: Vertical/Horizontal/Diagonal, p. 160

Figure A. Philip Pearlstein, ''Two Seated Nudes.''

Figure B. Hokusai, ''Yatsuhashi (The Eight-Plank Bridge),'' from *Views of Famous Bridges in Various Provinces.* 1833–1834. (The Metropolitan Museum of Art, New York; Rogers Fund, 1922)

Figure C. BeSong mask. Zaire, 19th–20th century. (The Metropolitan Museum of Art, New York; The Michael C. Rockefeller Memorial Collection of Primitive Art; Bequest of Nelson A. Rockefeller, 1979)

Figure D. Albrecht Dürer, ''Self-Portrait.'' 1493. (The Metropolitan Museum of Art, New York; Robert Lehman Collection, 1975)

C

D

Thomas Eakins, "Marey Wheel Photographs of George
Reynolds." c. 1884–1885. (Philadelphia Museum of Art;
Gift of Charles Bregler)

Movement

8

Introduction: Pictorial/Actual Motion

PICTORIAL motion is different from real movement. Although we may make a realistic image intended to be full of movement, we might actually come up with something that lacks any feeling of movement at all. For example, in **Fig. A** the camera has accurately recorded a horse galloping forward, but the resultant image has no forward movement at all. Rather, the horse seems to be galloping backward.

The photo by Clarence White **(Fig. B)** makes the same point in the opposite way. The subject is still: a figure, relaxed and self-absorbed, in a corner of a Victorian sitting room. Visual motion is everywhere, however, from the acrobatic swinging curves of the chaise lounge to the broken and fluttering shape of the figure's white dress.

The rocking chair in **Fig. C** is not an image in the sense that either of the two photos is, but it does beautifully convey the endless back and forth of the rocker's motion, even in a photo.

What is the relation, then, between moving things and pictorial movement? And how do artists control and organize the elements of an image to impart the liveliness and vitality of motion to static forms?

Figure A. Horse Race, newsphoto.
Figure B. Clarence White, ''Miss Grace.'' c. 1898. (Collection, The Museum of Modern Art, New York; Gift of Mrs. Mervyn Palmer)
Figure C. Gebrüder Thonet, ''Reclining Rocking Chair with Adjustable Back.'' c. 1880. (Collection, The Museum of Modern Art, New York; Phyllis B. Lambert Fund and gift of the Four Seasons)

A

B

C

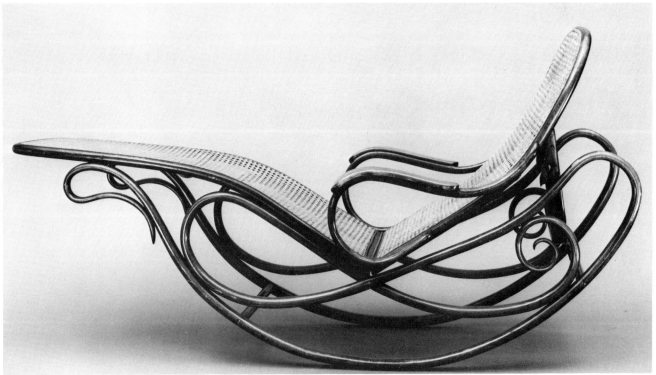

Directed Tension

Movement in a design does not necessarily have anything to do with a ''photographic likeness'' of a galloping horse or a bird in flight. We have seen that a quite accurate photograph of a form in motion can still look absolutely frozen. Movement in a visual pattern is not a result of subject matter but rather is *built into* the shapes, directions, and forms. The seeds of motion are already contained in the tensions that form every shape, line, or composition.

As long as the tensions and forces within a shape or composition are nearly equal, a sense of stillness and balance will prevail. For instance, in a square, the force of the horizontal is about equal to the lift of the vertical, and in an equilateral triangle the thrust of one point is approximately equivalent to the thrust of every other point. A stable balance is achieved (**Fig. A**).

Symmetry also creates stillness, and a form will seem more static when its main structural lines are vertical and horizontal. Diagonals tend to create visual movement. That is why the arrowhead shape of the triangle in Fig. A, stable as it is, seems more capable of movement than the square next to it.

When a regular or symmetrical shape loses its symmetry, or when the thrust of one direction becomes stronger than that of the others, the sense of energy or tension increases. In **Fig. B** the square has become an arena for tensions that pull it in every direction, and the circle, pulled in one direction, becomes like a taut rubber band, ready to fly when released. We can see this happening in the dynamic oval of the wheel and the stretched-out diagonals of the spectators in Jacques Lartigue's photograph in **Fig. C.**

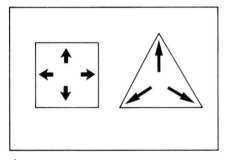

A

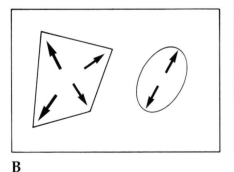

B

C

When increased tension is given a direction, when one force becomes a dominant axis, motion becomes stronger.

Tension plus direction equals motion in a design. Compare, for instance, the orderly stillness of a composition by Mondrian **(Fig. D)** with a similar design by Jean Arp **(Fig. E).** In the Mondrian, the vertical and horizontal grid holds each shape in its grip, and tensions within the shapes feel contained and controlled. Arp's composition, on the other hand, seems to stretch and swell with pictorial forces. The diagonals and the strong asymmetry of the shapes convey movement and a more unrestrained energy.

Also see: Tension, p. 20
Asymmetry, p. 24
Tension & Shape, p. 132

Figure C. Jacques Henri Lartigue, ''Grand Prix of the Automobile Club of France, Dieppe.'' 1911. (Collection, The Museum of Modern Art, New York; Gift of the photographer)

Figure D. Piet Mondrian, ''Square Composition.'' 1922–1925. (The Phillips Collection, Washington, D.C.)

Figure E. Jean Arp, ''Squares Arranged According to the Law of Chance.'' 1917. (Collection, The Museum of Modern Art, New York; Gift of Philip Johnson)

D

E

Gradients & Movement

A gradient is a gradual change in a visual quality, such as in the direction of a line, in size, in value, or in texture. What is most important is that the gradient changes gradually and evenly, leading the eye smoothly in small steps so it does not have to jump from one change to the next.

A gradient can be an effective way to create a feeling of movement, as it does in the Rococo coffeepot in **Fig. A.** The swelling and tapering shapes generate a series of lively movements and countermovements. If you cover the image with a piece of paper and then slowly uncover it vertically, you can see the pulsing effect of the shapes.

More than one kind of gradient can be used in the same design, and additional gradients increase the sense of motion. To the square in **Fig. B** we add gradients of direction, texture, and brightness, each one gradually adding to the animation of the shape.

In the Cubist painting in **Fig. C** the space is moved in and out by gradients of value, light and dark changes made by a tissue of small, even brushstrokes. Where the step-by-step change from lighter to darker is broken, making the eye jump from very dark to very light, the gradient is not perceived and we see a new space, adjacent to but not continuous with the rest.

The eye also tends to move in the direction of diminishing intervals, that is, in any gradient, even of different sizes, we tend to see a movement from the larger quality to the smaller one. In Georges Seurat's "La Grande Jatte" **(Fig. D)** we begin our visual exploration with the largest figures and meander through the middle-sized ones, finally to the smallest in the back. The intervals create a movement into the picture from front to back. Obviously for this reason gradients also help create movement *into* the picture plane.

Also see: Hierarchy & Subdivision, p. 28
Arabesque, p. 34
Space Cues: Gradients, p. 74
Tonal Gradients, p. 178
Volume Color/Film Color, p. 224

Figure A. Ephraim Brasher, "Coffeepot." 1760–1780. (The Metropolitan Museum of Art, New York; Bequest of A. T. Clearwater, 1933)

Figure C. Pablo Picasso, "Nude Woman." 1910. (National Gallery of Art, Washington; Ailsa Mellon Bruce Fund)

Figure D. Georges Seurat, "Sunday Afternoon on the Island of La Grande Jatte." 1884–1886. (Courtesy of the Art Institute of Chicago; Helen Birch Bartlett Memorial Collection)

A

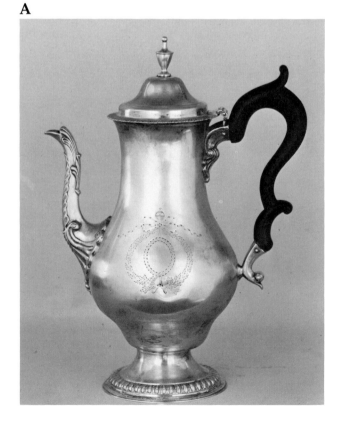

B

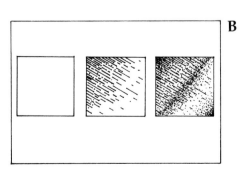

D

C

Vertical/Horizontal/Diagonal

THE degree of visual movement in an image often depends upon whether the lines, shapes, and other elements are placed vertically, horizontally, or diagonally. In general, the more vertical or horizontal the position of the shape, the more static or permanent it will appear. Conversely, the more it appears to lie on a diagonal, the greater the effect of motion and the more temporary the position looks. Compositions that are full of diagonals tend to look more dynamic than compositions dominated by vertical and horizontal elements.

The windmills illustrated in **Fig. A** all show equally possible positions for turning blades, but the first image feels frozen. The center windmill is more dynamic, but the ends of the blades are aligned on vertical/horizontal axes, forming an implied square. The blades of the last windmill appear to be moving most convincingly because of the more purely diagonal axes. The vertical and horizontal are neither evident nor implied.

When this simple principle is misused, the results can be almost comical. Peter Berhens' poster in **Fig. B** takes a dynamic image, a rearing horse and rider, for its subject. Rather than conveying motion, though, the image is stiff and frozen. Elements such as the horse's neck, the torso and arms of the rider, even the torch and flame that he holds, align with the vertical and horizontal.

Frances Johnston carefully posed her models for the photograph in **Fig. C.** The strong vertical accents that run through her composition create an image of measured stillness in which the figures have the monumentality and dignity of classical sculpture.

In the Japanese painting **(Fig. D)** verticals and horizontals are almost nonexistent. The see-saw and triangular pattern of the monkey's arms and the up-and-down constellation of circular heads seem like a time-exposure photograph of a bouncing ball. The twisted tree adds a further dynamic subtheme to this visually noisy composition.

Also see: Tension, p. 20
Asymmetry, p. 24
Isometric Perspective, p. 84
Line & Three-Dimensional Space, p. 150

Figure B. Peter Berhens, ''Poster for Deutsche Werkbund Exhibition.'' 1914. (Courtesy of the Library of Congress)

Figure C. Frances B. Johnston, ''Agriculture. Mixing fertilizer,'' plate from an album of Hampton Institute. 1899–1900. (Collection, The Museum of Modern Art, New York; Gift of Lincoln Kirstein)

Figure D. Attributed to Sesshu, ''Monkeys and Birds in Trees.'' 1491. (Courtesy, Museum of Fine Arts, Boston; Fenollsa-Weld Collection; 11.4141)

A

B

C

D

Stroboscopic Motion

WHEN objects similar in size or shape are placed in different positions in a progressive manner, we tend to see motion. In the poster in **Fig. A** the form of the dinosaur repeated three times creates a sense of a single dinosaur turning from left to right. The overlapping of the silhouettes increases the sense of three in one.

El Lissitzky's poster of ''1929'' **(Fig. B)** is another example of this kind of stroboscopic (revolving) effect. The two heads share one eye, and each head depends on the other to become complete. Irresistibly, the form flickers back and forth in a restless way.

When the number of shapes increases and a gradient is added, the sense of movement becomes even stronger. The pole-vaulting athlete in the photosequence made by Thomas Eakins **(Fig. C)** is part of a continuous and smooth gesture, and the repeated overlapping strengthens the dynamic effect.

Artists used this effect long before the camera or strobe light was invented. Pieter Breughel's ''Parable of the Blind'' **(Fig. D)** arranges a series of caped figures on the diagonal gradient of a hill. We move from a vertical figure on the left through increasingly diagonal figures, until we end on the right in a horizontal tumble. Echoing the fall of the beggars is a linear element, a series of sticks which jaggedly move from upper left to lower right. The figures are similar enough so that we can imagine each one as a separate ''still'' in a single motion.

A

B

Also see: Repetition & Variation, p. 30
Rhythm, p. 32
Color: Changes at the Edge, p. 210

Figure A. Ivan Chermayeff, ''Poster for the American Museum of Natural History.''

Figure B. El Lissitzky, ''USSR Russische Ausstellung.'' 1929. (Collection, The Museum of Modern Art, New York; Gift of Philip Johnson)

Figure C. Thomas Eakins, ''Marey Wheel Photographs of George Reynolds.'' c. 1884–1885. (Philadelphia Museum of Art; Gift of Charles Bregler)

Figure D. Pieter Breughel, ''The Blind Leading the Blind/Parable of the Blind Men.'' (Museo di Capodimonte, Naples)

C

D

Time

Seeing takes place in time as well as in space. When we see a ball roll across the floor, it moves through a period of a few seconds as well as moving from one side of the room to the other. In a drawing of the same subject, however, the world is entirely still. We have seen how the illusion of three dimensions can be presented in two-dimensional art, but how is the fourth dimension, time, dealt with in static images where there is no time? In the real world one moment is followed by another. In a drawing everything is seen simultaneously. How can we translate such motion into a medium where nothing moves?

A familiar way of describing a sequence of events is by dividing the page into smaller areas

A

and letting each area stand for a step forward (or backward) in time. Giotto's paintings illustrating the life of Christ are arranged on the walls of the Scrovegni family chapel in this way **(Fig. A).** Even when episodes take place over a number of years and at various locations, Giotto's scheme lays out the different events with tremendous clarity and simplicity. The one ground rule the viewer must follow is to look at the episodes from left to right, just as when reading.

This same method is used for comic strips. Leonard Dufresne's picture story uses a classic comic strip format to subdivide a brief happening into close-paced moments. Time here is experienced almost as it is in a stroboscopic photo. We see different, progressive aspects of the "same" action **(Fig. B).**

Figure A: Giotto, "Four Scenes from the Life of Christ: Ceremony of the Rods; Prayer for Miracle of Rods; Marriage of the Virgin; Wedding Cortege." c. 1304. (Arena Chapel, Padua)

Figure B. Leonard Dufresne, "Hamlet." 1980.

B

Jennifer Bartlett's work **(Fig. C)** uses the subdivided field, but no left-to-right sequence is laid out. We are free to imagine any sequence or none at all for the collection of units. The square-upon-square doesn't lead us in any particular way through time, but it does create a sense of additive time, separate moments which "add up" to a larger experience of seeing.

The image of many moments added up or compressed into a single space has been a basic theme for much art in the twentieth century. David Hockney's Cubist-inspired assemblage of Polaroids **(Fig. D)** captures something of the way we see things in time when we look. Looking takes time. The sensation of taking in all the visual events in our field of vision through many separate glances, all of them adding up to a

complex and flickering view of the subject, is conveyed by the accumulated subdivisions of the surface. In Hockney's work the simultaneous feeling of elements on a flat surface is a sort of advantage. The many layers of time become compressed onto the single layer of the picture plane, and the result is a more intense sense of the whole experience.

Also see: Rhythm, p. 32
Realism & Abstraction, p. 240

Figure C. Jennifer Bartlett, "2 Priory Walk." 1977. (Philadelphia Museum of Art; Purchased, Adele Haas Turner and Beatrice Pastorius Turner Fund)

Figure D. David Hockney, "David Graves, Pembroke Studios, London, Tuesday 27th April." 1982.

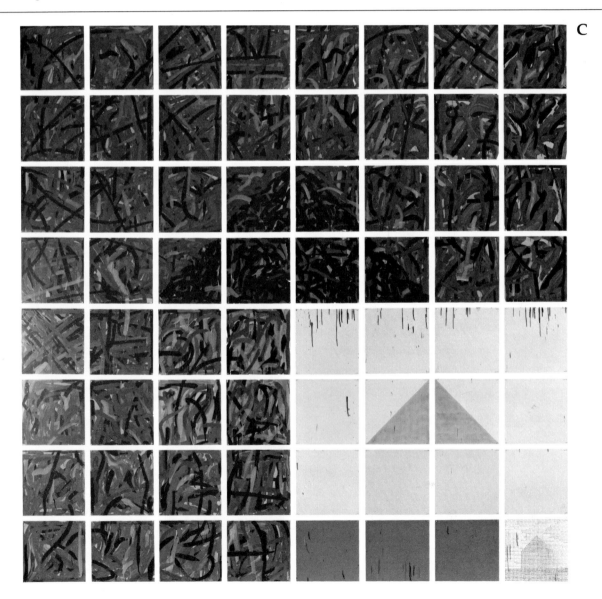

C

D

Claude Gellée (La Lorraine), ''View of a Lake.''
(Reproduced by Courtesy of the Trustees of the
British Museum)

Light

9

Introduction: Light Cues: Value

WHEN we speak of light, we are really referring to two different but interconnected qualities: color, and darkness or lightness, which we call *value*. Value without color refers to the range of grays from black to white. That is the type of value we will discuss in this chapter. Visual images, unlike the world itself, can be (and often are) made in media that have no range of color.

Gray, strictly speaking, is some combination of black and white (dark and light). A truly neutral gray is achromatic, that is, it has none of the redness, blueness, or yellowness of the colors on the spectrum.

Even though grays may lack the sensual impact of color, the range of grays can offer a wonderful means for generating the effect of light in an image. Grays can combine the almost liquid transparency of light flowing over forms with a severity and control that we usually find in drawing. Graphic designers, photographers, printmakers, and even painters find in the elegant unity of the gray scale a limitless potential for refinement, articulation, and drama.

A

The monotype by Edgar Degas in **Fig. A** is an image with a fluid light/dark composition. The glow of the footlights softens forms, washing like a phosphorescent wave over the figures and fading into the background, where only an occasional gleam or reflection remains.

The play of dark and light, the modeling of an illuminated form from light into shadow, is also the most straightforward means we have to render volume and mass. With a tonal eloquence not unlike that of the Degas, Eva Rubinstein's photograph in **Fig. B** uses the richness of the full gray scale to create shifting planes of light and to carve out volume and void, density and openness.

Also see: Elements of Color: Value, p. 188

Figure A. Edgar Degas and Ludovic Napoleon vicomte Lepic, ''The Ballet Master (Le maitre de ballet).'' c. 1874. (National Gallery of Art, Washington; Rosenwald Collection)

Figure B. Eva Rubinstein, ''Two Doorways, Palazzo Ducale, Sabbioneta, Italy.'' 1973. (Courtesy of the photographer)

B

Light Cues: Relative Value

W E make visual judgments by comparing one thing with another. We see a shape as large or small in relation to the size of the shapes that surround it. Similarly, color, direction, and shape can be affected by context. Value seems particularly subject to this kind of relative quality. In fact, we could almost say that our eyes understand value *only* in relation to its visual environment. This page appears to be white. So does a white refrigerator, and a white wall of a painted room, and a white rabbit's fur, but if these things were held up to one another, they would likely describe a whole range from light to darker.

In **Fig. A** the central gray strip bisecting the scale of grays is actually the same value for its entire length, yet it appears dramatically darker in the context of light grays and lighter in the context of dark ones. It is virtually impossible to see both ends of the strip as the same value without isolating them from their visual environments. When we arrange different values together in the same design, a mutual influence between tones becomes visible, with values looking darker on a light ground and lighter against a dark ground. As in any visual relationship, the smaller, subordinate value area will be most affected by the change, but the dominant or overall or ground tonality will be affected also.

In Georgio Morandi's etching in **Fig. B** the white still-life objects are the same value—simply the white of the untouched paper—yet they appear to be whiter, a kind of "super white," their value magically changed.

The same thing happens when we look at a line of type arranged on a surface that has variations of value **(Fig. C).** Not only is legibility affected by the changing degree of contrast, it is also affected by the way the value of the type itself seems to shift, becoming lighter here and

A

darker there. Change of this kind can be an enlivening element if used carefully, or it can become the source of an annoying lack of visual clarity which needs to be compensated for.

Also see: Relationships, p. 3
Color Interaction, p. 206

Figure B. Georgio Morandi, "Still Life." 1930. (Calcographia Nazionale, Rome)

B

C

Weight of Value

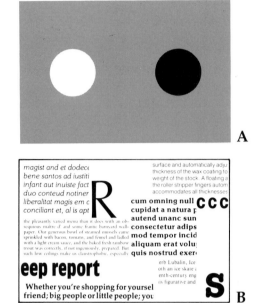

IN general, darker values are visually heavier than lighter ones. If two identical shapes are seen against the same ground, a black shape will tend to look weightier than one lighter in value **(Fig. A).** Darker value will tend to make a shape feel denser and more visually charged. Light values expand and pulse outward, just as light itself seems to radiate outward from a source. This effect, which can also be seen in the two circles of **Fig. A,** creates a slightly contradictory sense of expansion and contraction. The white circle seems larger, inflated with light, while the black one seems heavier and more compressed, but also smaller.

A visual texture, such as the weight of a typeface, creates darker and lighter areas in a design, and this light or dark effect can be enhanced by spacing. Lines of lightweight type with generous spacing between letters and lines will create overall light value areas, while a heavier typeface, closely spaced, will create darker areas, visually heavier and more dense. Therefore the artist using type can create light/dark compositions which use heavy and light forms as dramatic forces, and in which areas of text do more than just convey information **(Fig. B).**

A similar use of type as value, actually type-as-texture as value, can be seen in Picasso's collage/drawing in **Fig. C.** Large shapes made of newspaper text form middle value areas which contrast with the darker and lighter areas of the design.

Another kind of texture, the sometimes crowded and sometimes open scribble in the drawing in **Fig. D,** also creates dark and light,

dense and open areas. While the line itself remains uniform in its thickness and blackness, the varying concentrations of that line enable us to see a range of grays from heavy to light.

Also see: Top & Bottom, p. 48
Left & Right, p. 50
Weight of Shape, p. 130
Weight of Color, p. 212

Figure C. Pablo Picasso, ''La Bouteille de Suze.'' 1912–1913. (Collection, Washington University Gallery of Art, St. Louis)

Figure D. Henry Moore, ''Sheep'' from *Sheep Sketchbook.* 1980.

C

D

Value Contrast

As wide as the range is that the artist has to work with, the most extreme contrast from the blackest black to the whitest white doesn't approach the range of contrast that we see in the world around us. The artist merely creates equivalents to the effects of light that we experience when looking at the real world.

The effect of high contrast, widely separated values, is very different from that of low contrast, values from a limited section of the gray scale. We can see what these differences are in a schematic way by looking at the four configurations in **Fig. A.** The first uses the full range of value, from black to white. The second is in a light, or high key. It uses only values from one end of the scale; the lightest is white, the darkest only a middle gray. The third is a dark, or low key, limited to the dark end of the value scale, and the fourth is middle key, using a narrow range of value from the middle of the scale

A

B

C

but no values that are very dark or very light. In each diagram the shifting values define both the volumes and spatial relationships of the planes. In each the direction of the light source is clear, yet the different keys suggests particular kinds of light—from soft and hazy illumination to a muffled darkness, to the brightly lit feeling when the full range is used and we see the three-dimensional quality of the forms most strongly.

High contrast generally creates an image that is crisp and legible and in which three-dimensional qualities are enhanced. Less contrast may weaken these effects but offer other expressive possibilities, other ways of controlling emphasis.

The drawing by Lennart Anderson in **Fig. B** is low in contrast, this time in a light value range. This high key creates the effect of light reflected and air penetrating into every corner of the composition. The drawing itself feels almost as though we were viewing it through a screen of light.

Georgio Morandi's etching in **Fig. C** is composed with grays from the darker end of the value scale. The reduced contrast here creates a dark atmosphere which adds to the effect of density and heaviness in the composition.

The poster in **Fig. D,** on the other hand, achieves an image that is both clear and strongly three dimensional by using the two values representing the extremes of contrast—black and white—plus the mediating single middle value, thus creating the effect of strong light playing over solid forms.

Also see: Color Making Light, p. 216

Figure B. Lennart Anderson, ''Still Life with Mug and Coffee Filter.'' 1984.

Figure C. Georgio Morandi, ''Still Life with Coffeepot.'' 1933. (Collection, The Museum of Modern Art, New York; Mrs. Bertram Smith Fund)

Figure D. Jacqueline S. Casey, ''Body Language.''

D

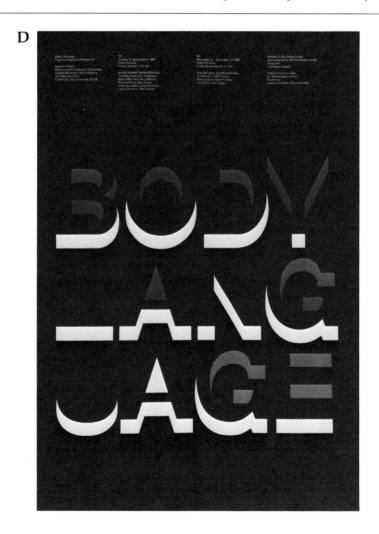

Tonal Gradients

WHEN we go from lighter to darker values in a series of more or less even steps, we create a *tonal gradient* which can lead the eye into and out of the depth or across the surface.

The abstract painting by Léger in **Fig. A** is built out of scores of small areas, each containing its own light-to-dark gradient. Each gradient creates a curved plane which tilts or bends into the picture space. If we eliminate the gradient in any of these areas and remake it with black and white as in **Fig. B,** we can easily see how the feeling of volume is diminished.

Rembrandt's landscape drawing in **Fig. C** shows space created by a gradient of value, a stepwise movement from light to dark in which forms seem to walk into the pale depths of the paper. A gradient of value used in this way is sometimes called *atmospheric* or *aerial perspective.* Whereas linear perspective systems use a set of precise rules involving vanishing points and diagonal lines to show how forms change size or location as they move further away from the viewer's eye, aerial perspective involves simply a basic perceptual understanding that colors and values become more similar with distance. This is a discovery that originated in landscape painting. Trees, hills, buildings, and other forms in the landscape tend to lose their color and value differences as they recede, as though being ab-

sorbed into an atmosphere, an effect that becomes especially notable on misty or rainy days.

The same kind of gradient is at work in Chris Rovillo's poster in **Fig. D.** Here the progressive change of value moves us gently into and then out of the space of the page as we move up the surface.

A beautiful example of a tonal gradient constructed to create the effect of light more than space is seen in Hannes Beckmann's painting **(Fig. E).** The careful control of both value change and contrast gives the image a luminosity which is not related to outside illumination or atmosphere, but which seems to radiate from the work itself.

Also see: Space Cues: Gradients, p. 74

Volume Color/Film Color, p. 224

Figure A. Fernand Léger, ''Village in the Forest.'' 1914. (Albright-Knox Art Gallery, Buffalo, New York; Gift of A. Conger Goodyear, 1960)

Figure C. Rembrandt van Ryn, ''View Over the Amstel From the Rampart.'' c. 1646. (National Gallery of Art, Washington; Rosenwald Collection)

Figure D. Chris Rovillo, ''Change.'' (Chris Rovillo, Richards Brock Miller Mitchell and Associates, Dallas)

Figure E. Hannes Beckmann, ''Plus Four-Red.'' 1965. (Courtesy of the Harvard Art Museums—Busch-Reisinger Museum; Gift, Mrs. Charles L. Kuhn in honor of Mr. Irving M. Sobin)

A

B

C

D

E

Value Creating Depth

W E can use value and contrast of value to create a feeling of depth in an image in a number of ways. We have already seen that a tonal gradient gives a sense of volume and mass, particularly in the modeling of rounded form. It is easy to see how a delicate and precise gradation of value enables us to see the beautiful spheric volumes of the head in the drawing in **Fig. A.**

A gradient can also be applied to many forms to create the effect of atmospheric perspective such as we see in a landscape drawing **(Fig. B).** Value used in this way can help us to read through deep or open space. More contrast pushes forms farther apart in space while less contrast draws them closer together.

We can define more formal, less literal kinds of space with value as well. Whenever different values are placed on a surface, they will seem to lie at different levels, at different distances from the picture plane. We can see this kind of space, moving gently in and out, frontal rather than curved, tilted, or atmospheric, in the detail of a Roman pavement mosaic **(Fig. C).** Here the arrangement effectively destroys the flatness we usually expect in a floor or sidewalk.

Value can create illusions of transparency. The effect of a film of light or dark is one of the more magical effects of value. By adjusting values that lie next to one another, the artist can make a unified light appear to play over forms. A simple rule must be followed: Whatever the film does to one area it must do to every other area that it covers; if it darkens or lightens one area to some degree, it must darken or lighten other areas to the same degree **(Fig. D).**

A film that decreases the light in an area, darkening it, is called *subtractive,* and one that lightens or appears to add illumination is called *additive.* In **Fig. E,** a painting by Paul Klee, we see a complex use of many kinds of transparency, additive and subtractive films, to create a space that has a lyrical, delicate, and dreamy quality without relying much on realist space.

A similar play between transparency and opacity, space and volume, can be seen in James Miho's advertisement for the Container Corporation of America **(Fig. F)** in which careful con-

A

B

trol of a limited number of value changes allows us to look both at and through objects and shapes in a design that alternates flatness with volume.

Also see: Surface Color, p. 222

Volume Color/Film Color, p. 224

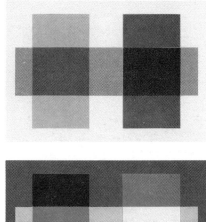

C

D

E

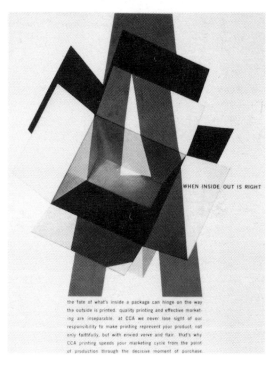

WHEN INSIDE OUT IS RIGHT

the fate of what's inside a package can hinge on the way the outside is printed. quality printing and effective marketing are inseparable. at CCA we never lose sight of our responsibility to make printing represent your product. not only faithfully, but with envied verve and flair. that's why CCA printing speeds your marketing cycle from the point of production through the decisive moment of purchase.

F

Figure A. J. A. D. Ingres, ''Study for the Portrait of Mme. Moitessier.'' c. 1844–1851. (Worcester Art Museum, Worcester, Mass.)

Figure B. Claude Gellée (La Lorraine), ''View of a Lake.'' (Reproduced by Courtesy of the Trustees of the British Museum)

Figure C. Pavement mosaic from the villa of Lucus Feroniae. Roman, 1st century A.D.

Figure E. Paul Klee, ''Green-Orange Gradation with Black Half-Moon.'' 1922. (Courtesy of The Harvard University Art Museums—Busch-Reisinger Museum; Purchase, Association Fund)

Figure F. James Miho, ''When Inside Out Is Right.'' (Courtesy James Miho and the Container Corporation of America)

Iranian Painting, ''The Court of Gayumarth.'' c. 1525–1535.
(Collection of Prince Sadruddin Aga Khan)

Color

10

Introduction

THE idea that we see by comparing is nowhere more evident than in a discussion of color. Not only do adjacent color areas dramatically affect each other, but color itself is created and understood only in comparison to other colors. We can truly say that there is no such thing as ''a color,'' only color relationships, comparisons between and among colors.

What is color? In the strictest sense, it is a range of visible frequencies of light, the components of a beam of white light which, when passed through a prism, breaks down into a spectrum of colors—red, orange, yellow, green, blue, indigo, violet, in a fluid progression **(Fig. A)**. Each color that we name and each gradation between has a particular frequency or wavelength, like the frequency of sound which determines pitch in music. When white light hits a surface, the surface will, according to its particular molecular structure, absorb some wavelengths of the light and reflect others. The color of this reflected light is the color we see **(Fig. B)**. If all of the white light is reflected, the surface will appear white; if all of it is absorbed, the surface we see will be black. In dimmer light, we see color less intensely. In a colored light, such as the red light of a photographic darkroom, the color of an object will appear changed (and, indeed, is changed).

Unless we are working with light itself as a medium (and some artists do), the colored medium with which we work—oil paint or printer's

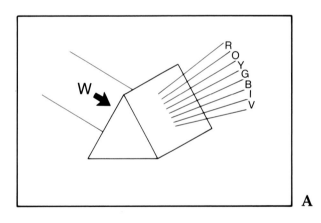

A

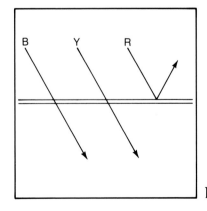

B

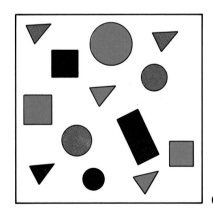

C

ink or powdered pigment or colored paper—is not color, it *has* color. It reflects and absorbs light in exactly the same way any surface does. We will discover that paint or colored media can behave differently from light. Still, artists have always been led on and fascinated by the way that colored materials can create a magical effect of light.

We probably notice color before we notice shape or form, and we respond to it intuitively and immediately. Speaking about a detail in a painting by Delacroix, Cézanne remarked that "the color of the red slippers goes into one's eye like a glass of wine and down one's throat."

We can see in **Fig. C** how color grabs us and asserts itself. We naturally group and organize separate shapes by color even when forms share other qualities, such as orientation, shape, or proximity.

There is a dramatic difference between a black and white and a colored image. What may be so compelling about black and white images is that they are inconsistent with our experience of the world, which is bathed in an extraordinary range of colors mixed in an infinite variety of combinations.

Also see: Relationships, p. 3

Elements of Color: Hue

THE quality we usually refer to when we identify a color is its *hue*, its redness or blueness or yellowness or greenness that locates it on the spectrum. Hue can be the aspect of a color's character that plays the most important role in a work of art, but as we will see, hue only partly describes what we see when we look at a color.

Our eyes can distinguish about 150 hues. Were we to divide the spectrum into 150 separate colors, we would be able to see each as slightly different from its neighbors. If, however, we divide the spectrum into, say, 175 different colors, each would visually blend with the color adjacent and we would see a smooth, continuous modulation. Of these 150 hues, some seem more important or memorable than others. The most basic are the three we call the *primary colors*, red, blue, and yellow, which are distinguished from the rest because they are the raw material from which all the other hues are formed. We can make orange by mixing red and yellow, or green by mixing yellow and blue, but the primaries themselves cannot be produced by any mixture. They are irreducible.

The second memorable triad of colors is the group resulting from the mixtures of the three primary colors: orange (red + yellow), violet (red + blue), and green (blue + yellow). These are called the *secondary colors* (or *secondary triad*). As we shall see, however, nothing about color is as simple as it seems to be. We do not perceive green, orange, and violet as having the same clear, balanced relationship that the primary triad does. Almost anyone can see that orange is made up of redness and yellowness, but most people have a more difficult time recognizing the components of green, which to some eyes seems to have the "pure" quality of the primaries. For this and other reasons, green is allowed as a fourth primary in some colors systems, while in other systems it is recognized as having a visual potency different from either orange or violet.

In order to visualize their relationships clearly, it is customary to arrange the primary and secondary colors and intermediate subdivisions into a circular chart called a Color Wheel. **Fig. A** is a simple version of such a wheel. Artists and theorists have over the centuries devel-

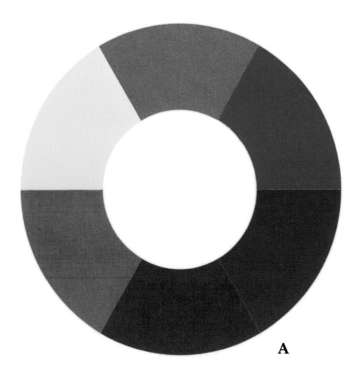

A

oped many beautiful variations of this wheel in an effort to present the colors in a way that is true to our perceived experience as well as to the physical qualities of color, that is, in an arrangement that is logical as a chart and that also makes sense to the eye.

European artists have for centuries debated the importance of color versus line and value. Most good Western artists have been adept at handling both color and drawing, but the power and impact of hue were restored to modern Western art by contact with cultures whose art made more use of hue, such as Arabic painting, or the simple and bright colors of ''folk art.''

The Arabic painting in **Fig. B** gives the eye some of the voluptuous pleasure that might be gotten from looking at a brilliantly colored butterfly. As carefully planned and finely drawn as it is, it is the radiance of the hues—their quality as purely visual events rather than as concrete descriptions of the colors of the objects in nature—that grabs and holds the eye.

Also see: Color Systems, p. 196
Color Interaction, p. 206

Figure B. Iranian Painting, ''The Court of Gayumarth.'' c. 1525–1535. (Collection of Prince Sadruddin Aga Khan)

B

Elements of Color: Value

Value, the range from dark to light, does not apply only to black and white. Every spot of color has a value. We can make a color lighter or darker in value by adding white or black to it. By raising or lowering the value of a color, we gain another whole color dimension and make color an even more flexible tool. The blue in **Fig. A** is made progressively lighter in one direction and darker in the other to produce a range from white to light blue to pure blue through darker blues to black. The hue itself, the "blueness" of the blue, is unchanged.

Some hues seem to keep their characteristics at very high or low values, whereas others seem to change when they darken or lighten. We think of red at a light value as pink rather than light red. Dark yellow looks more like olive green than yellow, yet blue remains blue whether it is dark or light. It is therefore clear that there is a psychological dimension to consider regarding color; we must finally make our color judgments and decisions through our eye rather than with charts or rules.

It is important to remember too that every *hue* has a specific value in its pure state. No color can be as dark as black or as light as white, but pure blue is darker than pure orange; yellow is lighter than green. If we arranged the color wheel according to the value of each hue, we would develop a simple curve, with violet as the darkest hue and yellow as the lightest. We might also imagine equivalents in value to each hue by placing each next to the gray of the same value on a graded gray scale **(Fig. B).** This is not easy to do. For instance, it can be difficult to align the strong character of yellow with the lightness of value we generally associate with soft pastels. Furthermore, yellow is so different in value from any of the other pure hues that we can easily become confused.

A work that is *monochromatic* uses only one hue and creates contrast by variation of value. The effect might be that of strongly colored light or of a thick atmosphere. In the painting by Edgar Degas **(Fig. C),** we can see how a near monochrome scheme creates a dramatic kind of illumination, different from the range of gray and also different from the full range of color. Here the use of a single color unifies elements and also enables us to react to the particular quality of a single hue.

Also see: Light Cues: Value, p. 172
Color/Value Range, p. 214

Figure C. Edgar Degas, "Madame Camus." 1869–1870. (National Gallery of Art, Washington; Chester Dale Collection)

A

B

C

Elements of Color: Intensity

THE third characteristic of color is its *intensity*, its brilliance or dullness (grayness). A hue is at its most intense in its pure state, when it has had neither black nor white added to it. Adding black *and* white (gray) or adding the color's *complement* (the color opposite it on the color wheel) lowers the intensity, making a color duller.

When a color reaches the lowest possible intensity, it is said to be *neutral* **(Fig. A).** A neutral has no chromatic quality at all, neither redness, blueness, or yellowness. Theoretically, a neutral is the same as a gray, but in practice we find that the neutral that results from a color mixture has a somewhat different presence than the gray made from black and white.

We tend to confuse intensity with value. Often in lowering the intensity of a color we lower its value as well, but the two qualities are not the same. In **Fig. B,** we see two pairs of colors. In the first pair the intensity is different but both are of the same value. In the second we see two colors of similar intensity, but one much darker, lower in value, than the other.

The average eye can distinguish about 200 distinct steps in value from black to white, before the steps visually blend into an even continuum. For most colors it can also distinguish about 20 steps in intensity, from the pure hue

to a neutral gray of the same value. In **Fig. C** the color becomes less intense (duller) but its value remains the same. Remember that the range from a higher to a lower intensity exists in the pure hues themselves. Yellow is more intense than blue, violet is not as brilliant as red.

Intensity is perhaps the most subtle of the three visual qualities that constitute a color, but it is also a wonderfully rich means for modulating color. In **Fig. D** we see the beautiful velvety quality of a color scheme in which all colors are of a fairly uniform low intensity. In **Fig. E,** on the other hand, we see the very different effect of contrast between very intense color and color of low intensity in the same image.

Also see: Space that Comes Out of the Picture Plane, p. 92

Elements of Color: Hue, p. 186

Elements of Color: Value, p. 188

Afterimage/Complementary Color, p. 194

Color Space, p. 218

Figure D. Geraldine Millham, Chairback Tapestry (detail). 1984. (Courtesy of the artist)

Figure E. Michael Vanderbyl, ''Six by Six.'' (Vanderbyl Design, San Francisco)

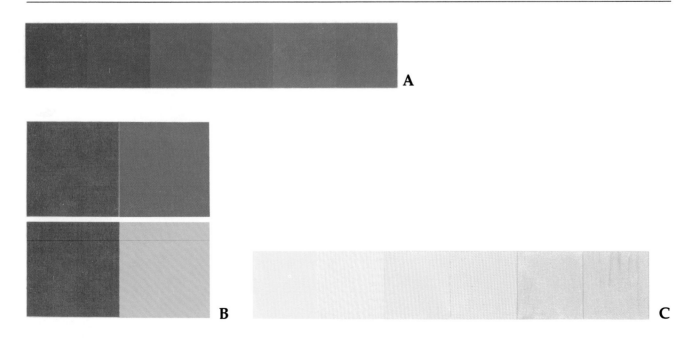

A

B

C

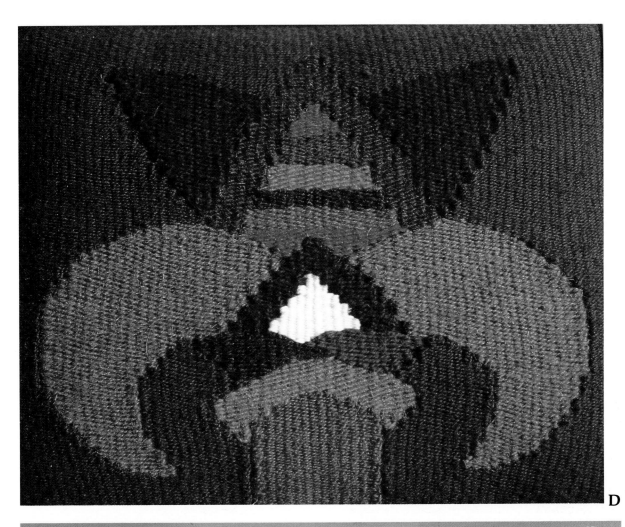

D

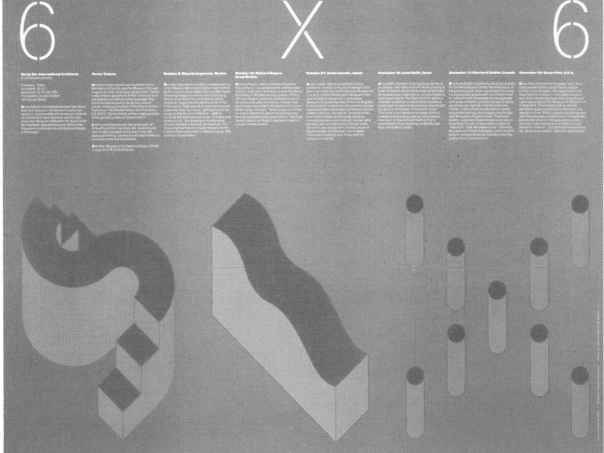

E

Color Temperature

THE hue, value, and intensity of a color are all reasonably measurable qualities. Color also has another dimension, a psychological one, that is difficult to measure but that we all intuitively feel and respond to. This quality is color *temperature*.

Colors can make us feel warm or cool. People coming from the cold into a blue-green room will not feel warm as quickly as they will entering a red-brown room of the same temperature. Pale blue seems an appropriate color for a swimming pool in which we want to cool off, but perhaps bright orange would not. "Icy" blue and "fire" red are certainly in part associations, but they also embody psychological and even physiological effects of color, less easily measured by instruments, but quite real.

Generally, most of us see the range from yellow through orange and red as warm, and the corresponding range from green through blue and violet as cooler **(Fig. A).** These perceptions can be affected by context and perhaps by personal temperament, but most people would choose red or red-orange as the warmest color and blue-green as the coolest.

Temperature is a useful tool when an artist is working without the full range of the color wheel. The painting by Edwin Dickinson in **Fig. B** uses warmer and cooler grays to create the impression of color. At the cool end of the scale are blue grays, at the warm end are brownish grays, and in between are a vast range of warmer and cooler neutral values, made from various proportions of blue, brown and white. The overall impression, while not the same as a full-color painting, gives a feeling of color beyond what a simple black-and-white palette can create.

Also see: Color Space, p. 218

Figure B. Edwin Dickinson, "The Cello Player." 1924–1926. (Jordan-Volpe Gallery, New York)

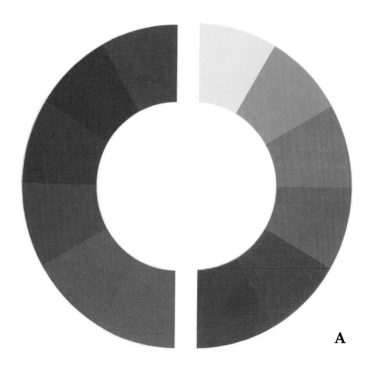

A

B

Afterimage/Complementary Color

STARE at the red dot in **Fig. A** for about 30 seconds and then shift your eye to the small black dot in the adjacent square. Most people will see a ghost image of a blue-green circle on a white field. This blue-green is the *complement* of the red, the exact opposite color quality. Where did this color come from? Simply, you have strained the color receptors for red in your eye by staring, and they now relax and compensate by ''calling up'' their opposite quality, much in the way we might restore our equilibrium with a cold shower after a hot sauna. A camera would not see the blue-green you are seeing, nor is there any way of recording it, but it is there for your eye none the less.

This phenomenon of a color generating an afterimage of its complement is sometimes called *successive contrast.* That particular blue-green ''manufactured'' by our senses is the exact natural complement of that particular red. Were we to continue this experiment with other colors, we would end up with a sequence of colors, paired by the extremity of their contrast, which we could arrange into a color wheel much like the one in **(Fig. B)**. These pairs represent absolute opposites which attract and repel one another like magnets and make tense and lively partners.

Another way to understand the kind of balance implied by complementary pairs is to mix together (with paint) complementary colors **(Fig. C)**. In each case—blue and orange, yellow and violet, red and blue-green—they combine to create a *neutral,* a ''color'' of no particular hue or temperature and of the lowest possible intensity. This neutral (equivalent to a neutral gray) is the balanced combination of absolute opposites, totally resolved. It is made up of all the colors of the spectrum (each pair contains red, yellow, and blue), yet it is without color. Some theorists believe we sense this calm resolution in all complementary pairs, even when they are as vibrant as red/blue-green, and in the similarly balanced triads of three primary or secondary colors, and for that reason find these combinations especially satisfying or pleasing.

Complementary colors have often been used as color schemes to organize works of art, and each pair of complements has a particular character. In Victor Moscoso's poster **(Fig. D)**

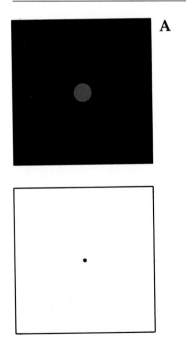

A

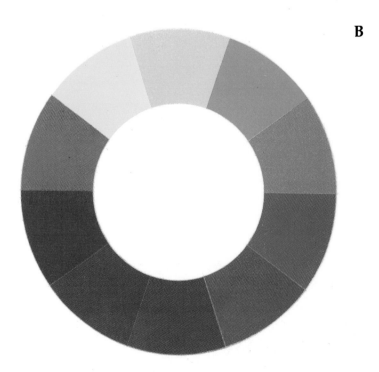

B

opposition of red-orange and blue-green, complementary colors of near equal value and high intensity, creates a visual vibration, an almost unbearable sense of tension between two strong colors. The eye is excited to the point of overload and the effect is one of electric intensity.

In the Van de Velde poster **(Fig. E)** the juxtaposition of a hot yellow with its complement, a low-intensity violet, seems instead like light and shade. There is heat here too, but it is the sunny vibrance of a tropical day.

Also see: Harmony & Dissonance, p. 204
Simultaneous Contrast, p. 208
Elements of Color: Intensity, p. 190

Figure B. Munsell-Color Circle.

Figure D. Victor Moscoso, ''Junior Wells and His Chicago Blues Band.'' 1966. (Collection, The Museum of Modern Art, New York; Gift of the designer)

Figure E. Henry van de Velde, ''Tropon l'Aliment le Plus Concentré'' (Tropon the Most Concentrated Nourishment). 1899. (Collection, The Museum of Modern Art, New York; Gift of Tropon-Werke)

C

D

E

Color Systems

W<small>E</small> can use a simple circle to organize color and make clear the basic relationships between red, yellow, and blue **(Fig. A),** but even that simple circle is vastly imperfect. What exactly do we mean when we say "red" or "blue"? Each of us probably calls to mind a slightly different image of each of these colors. Also what kind of chart would show how value and intensity can be arranged? Most important, even if one could devise such a scheme, what would be its use for artists?

There are a number of good answers to each of these questions. What do we mean by red or blue? Well, it depends. When light is passed through a prism and broken up into a spectrum, the colors that emerge are not exactly like the fire-engine red or deep sky blue of the color wheel. Instead, the red is a violet-red (sometimes called *magenta*), and the blue (called

cyan) has a greenish tinge. A color wheel in which these were the primaries would look approximately like the one in **Fig. B.** These primaries are also a printer's or a photographer's primaries: when printed as transparencies or as halftone dots, they produce the full range of color we see in color printing **(Fig. C).**

Fig. A looks more like the colors in our perceived experience—the "reddest" red, the "bluest" blue, and the "yellowest" yellow arranged in a triangular configuration, with even-looking gradations between. Color theorists have tried to modify this arrangement in order to take into account the various qualities of color in addition to hue. The color theorist Albert Munsell devised a color system based on optically correct complementary colors placed across from each other, and the whole extended into a lopsided solid in which hue, value, and inten-

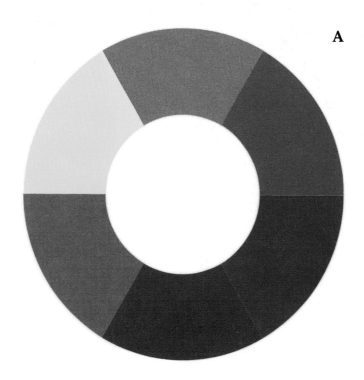

A

sity are accurately organized. This system is used by many paint, ink, and colored paper manufacturers **(Fig. D).**

William Ostwald developed a more subjective and "personal" color circle **(Fig. E),** which took the visual weight of color into account. For example, it gives more importance to green, which to him has an absolute or unmixed quality, almost a fourth primary. Also the range from red to blue is shortened. This system places more emphasis on the judgment of the eye than on the creation of a perfect and symmetrical system, and we see this subjective attitude reflected even in the color names.

An even more personal color chart is in **Fig. F.** This arrangement looks systematic, but as we move clockwise around the octagon, we see that the colors, which seem to be based on four primaries (red, yellow, blue, and green) include

four "secondaries": orange, a cooler red, then an almost black violet, and a greenish blue. This intuitive, slightly mystical approach to color reminds us again that any color system involves personal choices, and that, in the final analysis, if it looks right, it is right.

Standardized color systems have been used by printers, designers, and manufacturers of ink, paints, paper, and dyes to bring some order to a big range of hue/value/intensity. Products such as the Pantone color matching system replace the personal but imprecise language, such as "bone white" or "pinkish gray," with standardized and easy to find color choices. With this system a designer can choose a numbered

---

Figure B. Printer's primaries.

B

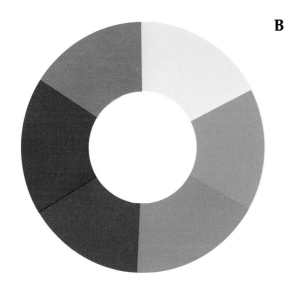

C

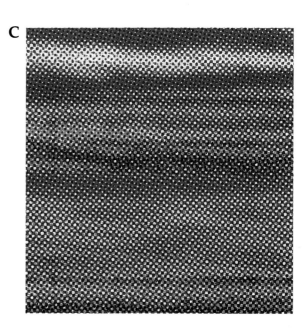

color and be sure that a printer using the same system will be able to match it exactly.

A systematic knowledge of how color ''works'' allows us to manipulate color in a thoughtful way, to use our conscious logic as well as our intuition. If a color seems wrong in our work, we can *imagine* the effect of making it darker or lighter, brighter or lower in intensity, warmer or cooler. We can be aware of different kinds of contrast and can anticipate how colors will affect one another. Knowledge eventually may become intuitive so we no longer rely on a system such as Munsell's, but the order of cause and effect which these color systems try to explain becomes part of our process of thinking as artists.

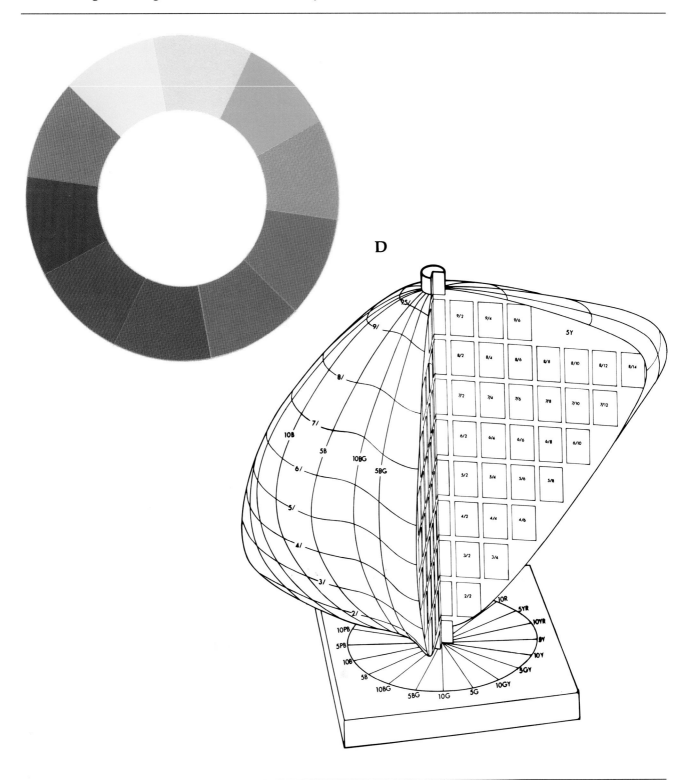

D

Figure D. Munsell-Color Circle. Munsell-Color Solid.
Figure E. Based on the 8 step Ostwald-Color Circle.
Figure F. ''Magic Square.'' Based on the Magic Square by Hermann Zapf.

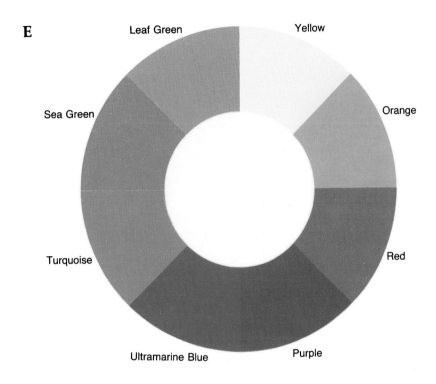

E

Leaf Green · Yellow · Orange · Red · Purple · Ultramarine Blue · Turquoise · Sea Green

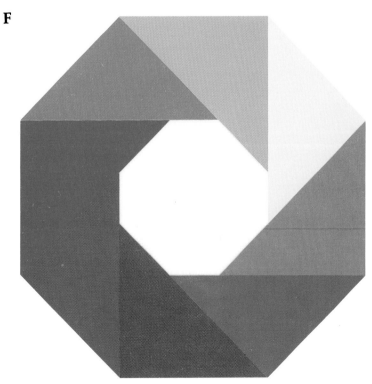

F

Color Mixing: Pigment Mixture (Subtractive)

We have already noted several results of pigment mixture. Mixing primary colors will produce the secondary and other intermediate colors. The value of a color can be raised or lowered by the addition of white or black. The intensity of a color can be lowered by the addition of its complement or of gray, and the careful mixture of two complementary colors or any symmetrical triad of colors (such as the three primaries or three secondaries) will produce a neutral, temperatureless gray.

Pigment—paints, pastels, or other colored materials—mixes in a way that approximates what is called a *subtractive* model. Imagine a series of colored films, transluscent plastics dyed red, yellow, and blue **(Fig. A)**. Each allows some light through and blocks other light frequencies. As we layer these films, we progressively eliminate more and more frequencies until no light can pass through. As we *add* colors, we *subtract* light. The combination of all colors is black, or the absence of light.

For a variety of reasons having to do with the way our eye and brain receive and interpret visual information, actual pigment mixes in a different way from our films. All the colors on a painter's palette combined do not produce black, but rather a dark neutral. Still, the principle is basically the same—more color, less light. Furthermore, pigments will combine to produce colors that do not appear on the spectrum of pure light—such as brown, ochre, olive green, and "metallic" colors, which all result from complex mixtures of several colors or materials.

This subtractive quality of pigment is the reason why a painter trying to make a picture of a blue car in golden sunlight will discover that adding yellow to the blue will make the car look not brighter but rather greener and less brilliant.

With pigment we can create illusions of true subtractive mixture, producing a rich sense of deep color space. We can see in the painting by Paul Klee **(Fig. B)** how "films" of color create illusions not only of transparency but also of the subtraction of light itself. A logical analysis of light and dark areas will not help us to untangle this evocative space, which creates its own tonal eloquence out of some very simple facts about how we see color.

Also see: Color: Introduction, p. 184

Elements of Color: Hue, p. 186

Elements of Color: Value, p. 188

Elements of Color: Intensity, p. 190

Color Space, p. 218

Figure B. Paul Klee, "Runner at the Goal, 105." 1921. (Collection, Solomon R. Guggenheim Museum, New York)

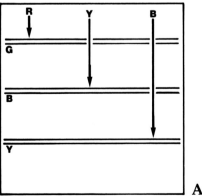

A

B

Color Mixing: Optical Mixture (Additive)

WE have already said that paint is not color, it *has* color. We see paint (or ink, or paper) as colored because it reflects only some of the wavelengths of white light sent out by the sun or other sources. Light itself, curiously enough, does not intermix in the way that pigment does.

Since all colors are components of white light, it follows that white light is the sum of all colors. If we project light beams of the three primary colors together, if we *add* light, the result will be a complete, white light. Even though this *additive* process of combining colors can be easily demonstrated, it is so different from our experiences with paint that it is difficult to believe.

Light mixes in other unexpected ways as well. It is based on a different set of primaries—red, violet, and green. Mix red and green light and the combination produces yellow light. In any combination, though, more color equals more light **(Fig. A)**.

Although beams of colored light are not the tools of most artists, paint can be used to create the illusion of additive color. In **Fig. B** a series of painted areas placed side by side create the appearance of a film of light. In order to create the illusion of an additive color film (one that uses color as well as value), we must be adjusting all the color dimensions—hue, value, and intensity. The basic rule is that whatever a film does to one color, it must do to any other color. If we have a color film then that lightens a blue background and makes it yellower, it will also lighten and make yellower any other background to the same degree.

Remember also that a colored surface gives off real colored light. Hold your hand close to a sheet of bright red paper, for instance, and it will turn slightly red in the reflected glow. Artists have tried to use this real reflected light as a creative element, too.

Since the middle of the nineteenth century, artists have been interested in the potential uses of true additive mixture, the mixture of real light. A flat circle, called a *Maxwell Disk*, painted with carefully controlled areas of red and blue-green will, when spun like a top, produce a white glow, which seems to float just above the surface, the result of mixing the reflected wavelengths of light. Artists who wished to obtain the brilliance and luminosity of colored light from pigment have experimented with applying color in fields of tiny dots which, when viewed from a distance, appear to blend; they allow the reflected light from the painted surface to mix in the eye, generating a lively transparent shimmer across the field. Painters like Seurat, who studied the science of color thoroughly, gave their pictures this special "real" light by using a dot technique, which came to be called *pointillism*. Since optical mixtures blend differently from pigment mixtures, there is always some element of the new and unexpected in the colors that are created at different distances from a field of dots. Notice the variation between the colors

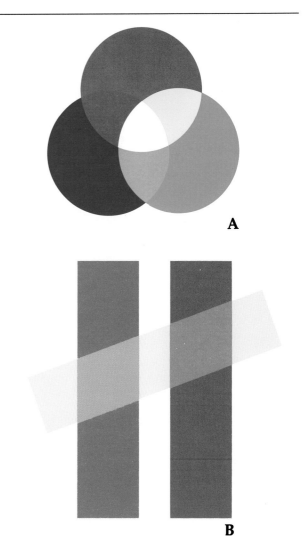

A

B

of the dots seen up close in **Fig. D** and the color glow that results when the same image is viewed from a distance in **Fig. C.**

This kind of color mixture has a special relevance to typographic design, where lines and columns of colored type may form a transparent field of color against a colored background **(Fig. E).** This "typographic pointillism" may affect how we see the color of the text on a poster close up and from a distance.

Also see: Value Creating Depth, p. 180
Color Systems, p. 196
Surface Color, p. 222

Figure C. Georges Seurat, "Seascape at Port-en-Bessin, Normandy." 1888. (National Gallery of Art, Washington; Gift of the W. Averell Harriman Foundation in memory of Marie N. Harriman)

Figure D. Detail of Figure C.

C

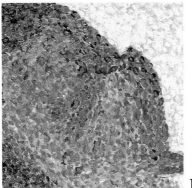

D

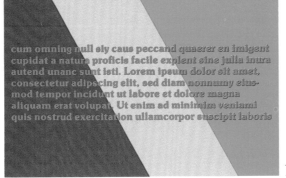

E

Harmony & Dissonance

MANY of the terms used to discuss visual art derive from music—*rhythm, interval,* even *key*. This sense of a similarity between the way we understand sounds and visual sensations is particularly evident in any discussion of color. Like music, color can be strongly emotive and expressive.

The idea of *harmony* has been applied to both music and visual art. Certain combinations, of either sound or color, seemed to have a special beauty or be intrinsically pleasing.

Colors that are near each other on the color wheel (sometimes called *analogous*) are usually defined as harmonious. So are colors of the same value, the same intensity, or both. A *monochrome* harmony describes colors of the same hue but of different values and intensities. We have already noted the special relationship of complementary colors or in symmetrical triads, particularly the primary and secondary triads. These and other arrangements of colors have long been thought to demonstrate clear visual relationships **(Fig. A).** The color theorist Albert Munsell developed a set of five colors, evenly spaced around his color wheel, all of the same low intensity and middle value, which he promised would always be harmonious **(Fig. B).**

In truth, harmony is not as simple as that. Were the world reduced to Munsell's five colors, it would be a dull world indeed. Furthermore, the way we see colors depends not only on the colors themselves, but also on the relative size of each color area, on the shapes that contain the color, and on the interaction between neighboring colors.

There is also the question of whether the traditional definition of harmony—resolution, calm, balance, everything falling clearly into place—is necessarily a useful or desirable goal in regard to color. Certainly dissonance, the opposite of harmony—the color that doesn't fit and that struggles to break out of the established order—is an enlivening and sometimes necessary element. *Dissonance* in color, as in music, is jarring, harsh, violent, or difficult. The aggressive language of dissonant color has been a potent device for artists, particularly in this century,

who wished to expand the emotional range and intensity of their work **(Fig. C).**

In fact, it can be argued that there is no such thing as dissonance at all, that dissonance and harmony are in the eye of the beholder. All the conceivable colors exist in nature, and some relationship exists among them all, if only the fact that they derive from the same simple spectrum. In a successful work of art, unity is achieved whether any particular rule of harmony is adhered to or not.

When color reinforces the expressively contorted drawing and bitter imagery of Kirch-

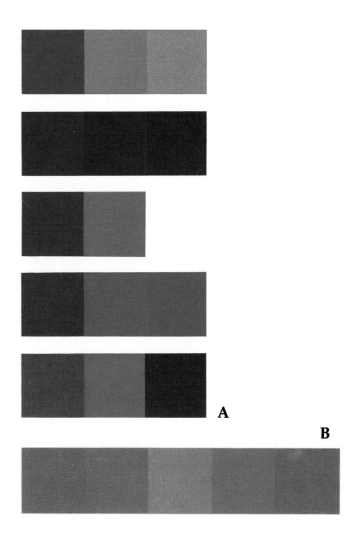

A

B

ner's ''Self-Portrait as a Soldier'' **(Fig. C),** or when it is muted and quietly harmonious as in the Corot landscape **(Fig. D),** it follows an internal logic.

Also see: Order, p. 12
Harmony & Dissonance, p. 16
Elements of Color: Value, 186
Color Systems, p. 196

Figure A. Monochromatic.
Analogous.
Complementary.
Split complementary.
Triadic.
Figure C. Ernst Ludwig Kirchner, ''Self Portrait as a Soldier.'' 1915. (Allen Memorial Art Museum, Oberlin College; Charles F. Olney Fund, 50.29)
Figure D. Jean-Baptiste-Camille Corot, ''River Scene with Bridge.'' 1834. (National Gallery of Art, Washington; Ailsa Mellon Bruce Collection)

C

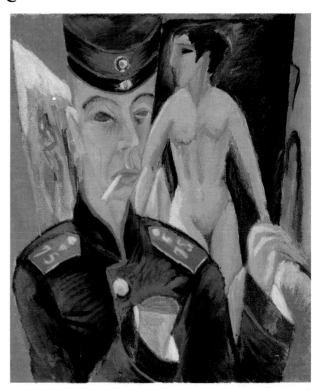

D

Color Interaction

W<small>E</small> have noted repeatedly that there is no such thing as a single and isolated color. Colors are always seen next to other colors. Even a colored dot on a sheet of paper will interact with the color of the paper—say, bright or dull white, buff, gray—and the two colors will change each other to some degree. When we speak of a color's hue, value, and intensity, we are describing that color in an imaginary void; when the color is placed in a context of surrounding colors, everything is changed.

We have seen how a gray appears to change dramatically when we alter the value of the field upon which it sits (Fig. A on page 172). An even more complicated pattern of interactions exists for color, with its many properties. The hue, value, intensity, and temperature of a color area are all affected by color interaction. In **Fig. A** a single, fairly neutral color is placed in four different color fields, and it changes its guise each time. Color interaction can make a single color appear hotter, cooler, lighter, darker, redder or bluer than it is. These color changes occur whether we want them to or not, so it is critical for artists and designers to understand just how colors interact and to anticipate those interactions. It is frustrating (and sometimes expensive) to mix a perfect tone for a particular purpose only to discover that it becomes a different color when applied to a white canvas or illegible when printed on green paper. The Italian Renaissance painter Titian must have recognized the importance of knowing how to manipulate the appearance of color when he bragged, as he supposedly did, that he could use mud to paint the flesh of Venus. What he meant was that if he could get a muddy, low-intensity color into the right relationship with surrounding values and colors, it would appear luminous, brilliant, and rich.

Probably the best-known systematic investigation of color interaction is found in the series of paintings by Josef Albers called "Homage to the Square." Albers chose the square as the most neutral format, neither too high nor too wide. He did not mix colors for these paintings, but used them straight from the paint tube, applying them smoothly and evenly and making

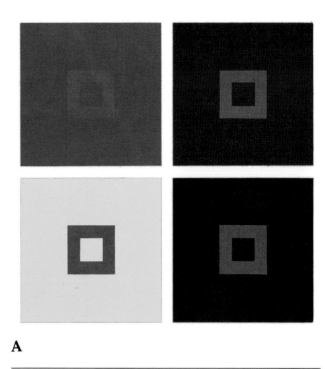

A

Figure B. Josef Albers, "Homage to the Square: Silent Hall." 1961. (Collection, The Museum of Modern Art, New York; Dr. and Mrs. Frank Stanton Fund)

Figure C. Josef Albers, "Homage to the Square: Apparition." 1959. (Collection, Solomon R. Guggenheim Museum, New York)

---

sure that no blank strip separated one color from another. There are no complex compositions in the series, and the square format of the outside is echoed within. Still, there is plenty to look at and work with. The size of the interior squares, the widths of the bands they create, and the hue, value, intensity, and temperature differences resulted in distinct and varied color personalities and kinds of light from one painting to another. A painting based on variations of orange might glow like a kiln. The opposition of blue and white might create the open and airy feeling of a Mediterranean landscape. Color might be made to feel compressed or expansive, edges made to seem crisp or dissolved **(Figs. B and C).**

Also see: Relationships, p. 3
Relative Value, p. 172

B

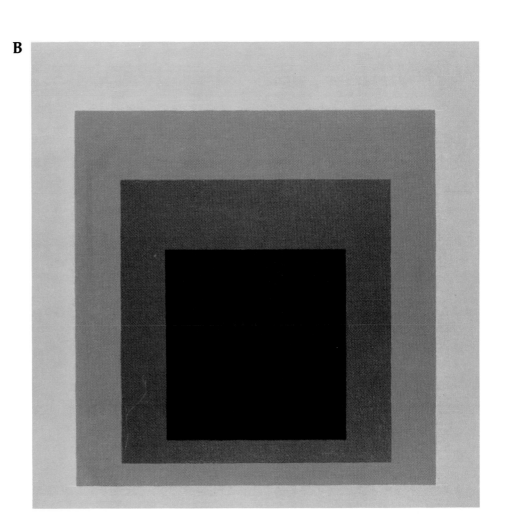

C

Color Interaction: Simultaneous Contrast

W E have already noted the effect of *after-image*, the ghostly image of a color's complement that one sees after staring at a color spot. When we look at colors that are next to one another, something similar happens. A black dot placed on a red field will look greenish, and placed on a green field it will look reddish **(Fig. A)**. The color of the field (say, red) will "call forth" its opposite quality (green) in a black dot placed upon it. This is something that happens in your eye and not on the page; if you peeled off the black dots, they would still be black. If you wanted the black dot to *look* black on a red field, you would most likely have to

make it a very dark red to compensate for the ghostly aura of green.

We call this effect in adjacent colors *simultaneous contrast*. The principle applies to all such interactions. A color will appear darker in value on a light ground and lighter on a dark ground, more intense on a more neutral ground and grayer on a very intense ground **(Fig. B)**. Green will look more yellow on a field of blue and more blue on a field of yellow **(Fig. C)**.

The effect, furthermore, is modified or enhanced by the particular colors chosen. Pure, intense, primary hues are not much affected by context, but lower-intensity colors and colors

A

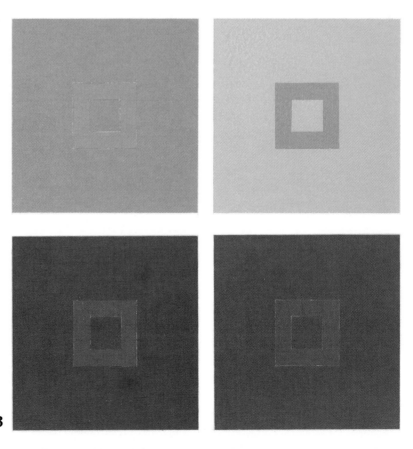

B

that are not primary or spectral can change appearance radically.

Size can also influence the effect of simultaneous contrast. Generally, larger color areas have more influence on smaller color areas. The small green square is changed by the color of the yellow or blue field, not the reverse. This is why colored type seems to be affected by the color of the ground and not the reverse, or why a red thread running through a green cloth looks so brilliantly red. Although we are usually not conscious of this "optical illusion," it is something we continuously experience in our ordinary perception of things. We do not see it happen un-

less it is presented in diagramatic form as in the figures here. The effect of simultaneous contrast is only interesting to the viewer of a work of art or design, but absolutely critical to its maker.

Also see: Relative Value, p. 172

Value Contrast, p. 176

Complementary Color/Afterimage, p. 194

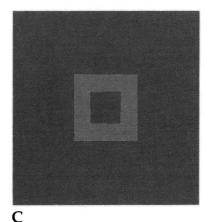 

C

Color Interaction: Color Interpenetration/Changes at the Edge

COLOR interaction—effects of simultaneous contrast, color vibration, and value change—happens most strongly where one color area touches another. If you look at the diagrams on the previous pages, you will notice that the color change is a bit more dramatic along the edges of the small rectangles, and the interior of a color area is somewhat different from its edges.

If we show a progressive color change on a row of bars **(Fig. A),** those shifts at the edges become even more apparent, giving an appearance of modeling, as though we were looking at a row of cylindrical tubes rather than flat bands. As you look from left to right the colors appear darker and bluer at the outer edge, and when you look from right to left the outer edge of each color appears to be lighter and more violet. In

A

B

other words, each edge seems to resemble the color on its *opposite* side rather than its adjacent side.

The crispness or softness, decisiveness or vibration, clarity or ambiguity of an edge can be as much a result of color interaction as it is of line or technique. High-intensity colors, particularly when they are of equal value and complementary hue, fight for visual dominance, and the result of the struggle is an edge that vibrates electrically **(Fig. B).**

If color areas are separated by a zone of white or black, they will keep their brightness but the intense vibration is eliminated. This is what happens in the painting by Leland Bell in **Fig. C.** Colors of a similar low intensity or value will join to form a soft edge which flickers in a gentler way **(Fig. D).** The cleanest, sharpest, and brightest edge will be seen between colors whose hue, value, *and* intensity are clearly contrasted **(Fig. E).**

Also see: Line as Edge: Contour Line, p. 146
Line as Edge: The Shifting Edge, p. 148
Value Contrast, p. 176
Elements of Color: Intensity, 190
Color Interaction, p. 206

Figure B. Stuart Davis, ''Owh! in San Pao.'' 1951. (Collection of Whitney Museum of American Art; Purchase; Acq. #52.2)

Figure C. Leland Bell. ''Dusk (I).'' 1977.

Figure D. Donald Guy Kaufman, ''Plink II.'' 1968. (Hirshhorn Museum and Sculpture Garden, Smithsonian Institution; Gift of Joseph H. Hirshhorn, 1972)

Figure E. Robert Jensen, Poster for ''Lutsen Design Conference.''

C

E

D

Weight of Color

Generally, darker colors are heavier looking than lighter colors, and they lose weight as they become lighter in value. Beyond this general rule, the artist's eye must make final decisions about color weight, and these decisions may be tiny.

For example, Otl Aicher's constructional drawing for the emblem of the International Olympic Committee is made up of five rings **(Fig. A),** each of a different color, value, and intensity. Each ring is given a particular thickness that compensates for the weight of its color. The black ring is thinnest, while the yellow ring is noticeably thicker. Reproduced in color, the rings seem equally weighted.

Intensity alone also creates differences in visual weight. In the painting by Wolf Kahn **(Fig. B)** large areas of pale lavender and silvery green are balanced by a small rectangle of black and an even smaller patch of intense yellow, the value of which is quite similar to the large areas of low-intensity color.

Also see: Balance, p. 18
Weight of Shape, p. 130
Weight of Value, p. 174

Figure A. Otl Aicher, International Olympic Committee Emblem.
Figure B. Wolf Kahn, "The Yellow Square." 1980.

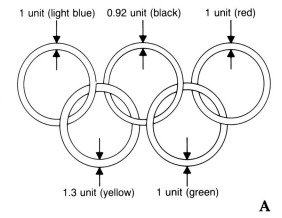

1 unit (light blue) 0.92 unit (black) 1 unit (red)

1.3 unit (yellow) 1 unit (green)

A

B

Color-Value Range

N a piano we can play the same tune at different places on the keyboard. If we use lower notes, the tune will sound heavy and rumbling, whereas a version high up on the keyboard will tinkle and sound brighter. Similarly, a range of color-value can be seen as a color keyboard, a scale from colors that are light in value and low in intensity to darker, more saturated or intense hues at the other end. A design can be put together in different color-value ranges or color keys **(Fig. A).**

Fig. B is an image based on a light-value, low-intensity color scheme. The brightest color is a fairly dull rose, but used only in small amounts across the top of the picture. The dark accent of the hair makes the larger areas of ivory and warm ochre seem even lighter. Together the color spots make a pale, luminous atmosphere, with a gentle phosphorescent glow.

In any color key, high or low, there will be a dominant note, one or two colors which become the central color motif in the composition. In **Fig. B** the dominant note is an ochre-ivory.

The darker, more intense green and orange of Georgio di Chirico's painting in **Fig. C** is a visually heavy, almost oppressive color scheme. The low key creates a loaded and gloomy atmosphere, one that is a recurrent fixture in the work of this Italian surrealist.

Also see: Value Contrast, p. 176
Weight of Color, p. 212

Figure B. Sheila Metzner, ''Evyan-towel, 1982.''
Figure C. Giorgio de Chirico, ''The Song of Love.'' 1914. (Collection, The Museum of Modern Art, New York; Nelson A. Rockefeller Bequest)

A

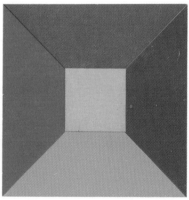
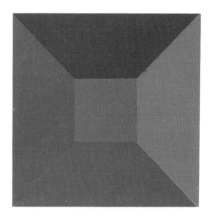
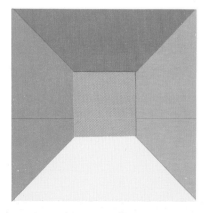

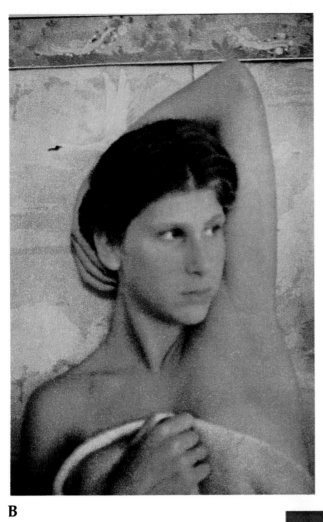

B

C

Color Making Light

A

I N visual art a shape, color, or form must appear to interact with other shapes and forms around it in order to avoid seeming visually isolated and dead. The color interaction that creates the illusion of light is one of the most marvelous examples of this principle. The appearance of light when areas of color are placed side by side becomes a mysterious ''fifth element'' beyond hue, value, intensity, and temperature.

Light in a design may be specific, like the fading warmth of a Cape Cod summer evening in Paul Resika's painting **(Fig. A),** or the light may belong to no particular time of day or weather.

Some artists are known for the quality of light that seems to appear in their work again and again. It is not unusual to hear references to ''Edward Hopper's light,'' the bright sunlight found in many Hopper paintings, or to ''Willem DeKooning's light,'' for the trembling, watery-looking and color-loaded brushstrokes in DeKooning's abstract expressionist pictures.

B

For light to be convincing in an image, it must be consistent throughout. For example, in a painted figure, a model bathed in light and shadow, different colors need to be mixed for the light side and the dark side of the face. The overall color quality of the face, such as fair skin or dark complexion, will come through in both the light and dark sides. Rather than thinking that the model is actually multicolored, we see a constant skin color bathed in a changing overlay of light and dark **(Fig. B).**

Figure A. Paul Resika, ''Provincetown Pier, for Joseph di Martini.'' 1985. (Private Collection; Courtesy of Graham Modern Gallery, New York City)

Figure B. Henri Matisse, ''La Coiffure.'' 1901. (National Gallery of Art, Washington; Chester Dale Collection)

Also see: Introduction: Light, p. 170
Local Color, p. 220

Color Space

ALL other things being equal, some colors tend to seem visually closer to the viewer than others. For instance, cool colors such as blues tend to recede into pictorial space, while warmer hues such as reds and oranges tend to come forward. All rules having to do with color, however, can be bent by an artist who is skillful enough. An intense electric blue will seem to be in front of a dull brownish red if the intensities and the sizes of the color areas are correctly balanced against one another.

The point here is that interaction between colors will create three-dimensional space on a surface even when perspective or shading is absent. Ivan Chermayeff's arrangement of colored tickets has an in and out rhythm that occurs as each color area finds its own level in front of or in back of its neighbors **(Fig. A)**.

The fact that colors can be used to make space seem deep or shallow, thus creating structure and a sense of three dimensionality, is an important tool. Whereas a Renaissance artist might have divided the construction of a painting into three distinct steps—drawing, shading with light and dark, and coloring—a modern painter like Paul Cézanne **(Fig. B)** realized that as color becomes richer, forms become more solid looking. Cézanne's forms are built of small bricklike dabs of color, each spot clear and definite, even in the leafiest or most atmospheric areas of a landscape. Thus in the single operation of putting down a paint spot, he combines three classic ways of creating three-dimensional form on a two-dimensional surface—careful drawing, light and shade, and color.

The process of getting the drawing right and then filling in with color is replaced by a kind of drawing with color. Color spots can be used by themselves (as they are in Howard Hodgkin's composition in **Fig. C**) to carve out points, planes, and distances in space.

Also see: Figure/Ground, p. 70
Gradients, p. 74
The Pictorial Box, p. 86
Space that Comes Out of the Picture Plane, p. 92

Figure A. Ivan Chermayeff, "International Design Conference, Aspen 1973." (Ivan Chermayeff, Chermayeff & Geismar Associates, New York)

Figure B. Paul Cézanne, "Houses in Provence." c. 1880. (National Gallery of Art, Washington; Collection of Mr. and Mrs. Paul Mellon)

Figure C. Howard Hodgkin, "Goodbye to the Bay of Naples." 1980–1982. (Private Collection)

A

B

C

Local Color

A N object's *local color* or *object color* is the color that we see in clear daylight, that is, in a neutral, white light. It is not, however, always the color that we see. A white cup may look red in the reflected glow of a red tablecloth, and a white building will turn pink in the sunset. Nevertheless, we call the cup and the building "white." In a strict sense, the reflected color of an object *is* its color. The fact that the coffee cup might be drawing its redness from the tablecloth doesn't change the way it looks to the eye. Even in "clear daylight," a white cup will take on a bit of the blueness of the sky, for instance.

All objects, regardless of their local colors, will take on some color from the surrounding world, but more intensely colored objects tend to be less easily influenced by environment. A bright green, for example, would have to be bathed in a strong red light before its greenness would disappear. Even then, it would tend to look brown rather than surrendering to the influence of the red light. A pale blue or a white, on the other hand, would be more changeable.

When we employ shapes with strong local color—reds, blues, and yellows—we get a sense of different qualities being fitted together, and there is some visual tension in this harmony of differences. The individuality of strong local colors may threaten the visual teamwork needed to make a total composition. At the same time, the color differences and contrasts are food for the eye.

Local color is largely what we see in the painting by Mantegna in **Fig. A.** The red, yellow, and blue areas are clear and straightforward. The light that bathes the figures has no color of its own and allows each of the bright

A

notes of the costumes to make its own contribution.

Fig. B also uses local color in a composition of distinct color personalities used partly for their eye-grabbing impact. The harmonies and dissonances create a family of exciting differences. Here we can still use the term ''object color'' as long as we realize that the objects in question are colored shapes.

In the painting by Bonnard **(Fig. C),** local color all but disappears. The whole is bathed in a richly colored light that pours across and through objects, walls, and the figure. The object color of each form is hardly visible under the impact of the flood of colored light.

Also see: Color: Introduction, p. 184

Elements of Color: Hue, p. 186

Figure A. Andrea Mantegna, ''Judith and Holofernes.'' c. 1490. (National Gallery of Art, Washington; Widener Collection)

Figure B. Paul Rand, ''Logo for NEXT Computers.'' 1986/1987.

Figure C. Pierre Bonnard, ''Nude in Bathtub.'' c. 1941–1946. (The Carnegie Museum of Art, Pittsburgh; Acquired through the generosity of the Sarah Mellon Scaife family, 70.50)

The sign of
the NeXT generation
of computers...
for Education

B

C

Surface Color

Surface color is color that you look at. It is anti-illusionistic. It does not try to create the effect of depth, or of sunlight in a landscape, for instance. Red or blue or gray is meant to be seen as real red or blue or gray arranged on a flat surface.

The straightforward impact of surface color is seen in Frank Stella's painting in **Fig. A.** Each color area is as literal as paint on a wall or an automobile fender. The radiance and ordinary beauty of red or yellow are given an extraordinary presence by its large-scale treatment.

In **Fig. B,** flat areas of color lay squarely on the surface of the sculpture. Here the literal quality of surface color reinforces the physical presence of the three-dimensional form.

Jasper Johns uses color to make a point about surface in his painting in **Fig. C.** His "Three Flags" is a "realistic" painting of a well-known object. It is also "real" in a literal sense,

that is, it is meant to be seen as flat color areas applied to a surface. Here surface color is used to set forth a paradox about the art of depiction and imitation, a meditation on what is "real" about an object and what is "real" about a painting.

Also see: Picture Plane, p. 56
Realism & Abstraction, p. 240

Figure A. Frank Stella, "Darabjerd III." 1967. (Hirshhorn Museum and Sculpture Garden, Smithsonian Institution)

Figure B. Jean Arp, "Enak's Tears (Terrestrial Forms)." 1917. (Collection, The Museum of Modern Art, New York; Benjamin Scharps and David Scharps Fund and Purchase)

Figure C. Jasper Johns, "Three Flags." 1958. (Collection of Whitney Museum of American Art; 50th Anniversary Gift of the Gilman Foundation, Inc., The Lauder Foundation, Mr. A. Alfred Taubman, an anonymous donor and purchase; Acq. #80.32)

A

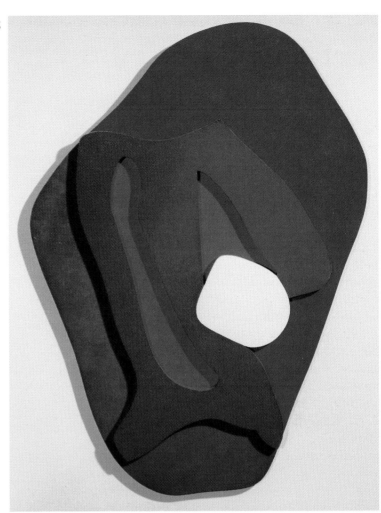

B

C

Volume Color/Film Color

A

ATMOSPHERIC or *volume color* is color you look *into*, color that makes space. Objects located in deep space lose their brightness as they get further away, and their color tends to become more like the background.

Color used as an atmosphere can create an especially illusionistic space, particularly when combined with perspective or size change. In Claude Monet's painting in **Fig. A** the shifting hues of the color seem to absorb form into distance.

We can also look *through* color, as if through a series of translucent films. When color areas are juxtaposed and carefully adjusted, the illusion of transparency can create another kind of deep color space.

Transparency makes forms visually lighter, dematerialized. Just as a glass wall in a building opens the structure to the eye, color used in this way allows the eye to move through color planes rather than across them. This feeling of light and air is exploited by John Marin in **Fig. B**. In Richard Estes' painting in **Fig. C** films are used to create a space of many layers. The transparency here turns the entire painting into a light-filled maze.

The basic logic for creating the effect of transparent color is that whatever a transparency does to one color it must do to any other color. A piece of pink cellophane laid over red, white, and blue will add the same amount of redness to each color, so red will become redder, white will become pink, and blue will turn violet **(Fig. D)**. A transparent gray over yellow, red, and orange **(Fig. E)** again needs its own special adjustments to make the illusion convincing. Here the gray turns the yellow into a gray-green, the red to a sort of brown, and the orange into a more neutral greenish color. Artists working with painted areas, rather than with colored films, have to use their eyes along with their knowledge of how color and light mix, to adjust each area so that it shares an equal amount of the added color with its differently colored neighbors.

Also see: The Pictorial Box, p. 86
Value Creating Depth, p. 180
Subtractive Color, p. 200
Additive Color, p. 202

B

C

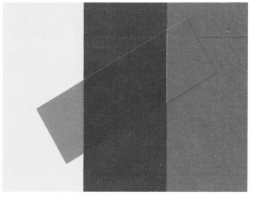

D

E

Figure A. Claude Monet, ''Waterloo Bridge, London, at Sunset.'' 1904. (National Gallery of Art, Washington; Collection of Mr. and Mrs. Paul Mellon)

Figure B. John Marin, ''Maine Islands.'' 1922. (The Phillips Collection, Washington, D.C.)

Figure C. Richard Estes, ''Double Self-Portrait.'' 1976. (Collection, The Museum of Modern Art, New York; Mr. and Mrs. Stuart M. Speiser Fund)

Descriptive Color/Subjective Color

A

ARTISTS often use descriptive color, that is, color mixed to match the color perceived by the eye. The ability to distinguish between subtle color differences is an important skill. The beginning student, with an untrained eye, may have trouble seeing the difference between, say, a cold blue-green and the slightly yellower emerald green, or between the blackish green of a pine tree and the green-brown of grass. The ability to see color precisely is useful both for realist painting and for working with nonobjective forms and shapes.

Of course descriptive color can include both local color (the color of objects outside of any context of colored light or reflection), and also the many color changes that result from light,

reflections, and other interactions with a colored environment.

It is impossible to match the entire range of color in nature with a colored medium like paint. Paint's range of value, for example, goes only from black to white, whereas nature's range goes from black to sunlight, a span many times greater. Descriptive color, as seen in the beautiful landscape by Monet **(Fig. A),** is often made by adjusting, simplifying, and exaggerating in order to create something that appears neither adjusted, simplified, nor exaggerated.

Subjective color, on the other hand, as seen in the landscape by Derain **(Fig. B),** is not bound by the appearance of things in the real world. Here colors are obviously exaggerated or

B

changed in response to forces that are not objective, and the artist is using the color itself as an expressive device to be consciously manipulated and to carry the meaning of the work, in this case an image of explosive agitation.

Working this way may be advantageous or disadvantageous, depending on the temperament and goals of the artist. Some artists feel that restrictions (such as having to match colors) force them to be more inventive. Others prefer the unlimited possibilities that they see in a more subjective approach. Although we may think of subjective color as "personal" and expressive compared with the "impersonal" color-matching of descriptive color, each approach is, of course, expressive of a certain way of seeing. The Monet is predicated on a sort of mutual understanding between the artist and the viewer: that there is something about the look of a landscape that we can all agree about. To paint a tree bright red under a blue sky would violate that sense of common ground.

Figure A. Claude Monet, "Argenteuil." c. 1872. (National Gallery of Art, Washington; Ailsa Mellon Bruce Collection)
Figure B. Andre Derain, "The Turning Road." 1906. (The Museum of Fine Arts, Houston; John A. and Audrey Jones Beck Collection)

Also see: Local Color, p. 220
Realism & Abstraction, p. 240

Much of the work that artists do with color is nondescriptive by its very nature. The designer or the typographer, for example, is more likely to use color as an object, part of an ensemble that will please the eye, organize information, create emphasis, or increase legibility and at the same time be expressive. The choice of colored paper for a poster, or the choice of color for type, may be determined by the internal needs of a composition and therefore happen in the eye of the artist rather than as the result of a give and take with an outside reference point, as in Monet's landscape.

Color Symbolism

Wᴇ tend to attach symbolic meanings to colors, seeing colors as standing for certain emotions or states of mind. For example, in our culture red is considered a color of anger or passion, and white symbolizes purity. These as-sociations seem logical to us. Other cultures, however, may make totally different connections in regard to color symbolism. For example, in China white is traditionally the color of mourning, worn at funerals as we would wear

A

black. The traditional colors of a monk's habit in the West are brown or gray, understood to be colors of quiet meditation, but Buddist monks, no strangers to meditation, wear orange or saffron robes. The yellow that we associate with warmth and the sun in so many Van Gogh paintings was the color of the six-pointed stars which marked the clothing of persecuted Jews in Hitler's Germany.

Some color theorists and artists, like the Expressionist painter Wassily Kandinsky, believed that specific associations can be made between the way we experience color and other sensory experiences. Kandinsky wrote that ''many colors have been described as rough or prickly, others as smooth or velvety, so that one feels inclined to stroke them'' (such as deep, brilliant blues; intense, cool greens; and dark red-violet). ''Some colors appear soft'' (rose or pink), ''others hard'' (cool, whitish greens), ''so that fresh from the tube they seem to be 'dry.' . . . The sound of colors is so definite that it would be hard to find anyone who would express bright yellow with base notes, or dark lake [rose] with the treble.''

Some of these observations have to do with color qualities that we can all agree exist—like temperature, weight, and so forth—others seem more like personal or poetic responses to color. It is difficult to separate the truth of such subjective perception from associations that might be learned. It may be that the expressive power of colors is not in the colors themselves, but in the combinations and interactions that we can create among them **(Fig. A).**

Perhaps the most that can be said about assigning meanings or emotions to specific colors is that it has always interested artists and that it certainly has a use in communicating to an audience with a shared idea about what meanings are attached to which colors.

Also see: Signs & Symbols, p. 238

Figure A. Paul Klee, ''Fire at Evening.'' 1929. (Collection, The Museum of Modern Art, New York; Mr. and Mrs. Joachim Jean Aberbach Fund)

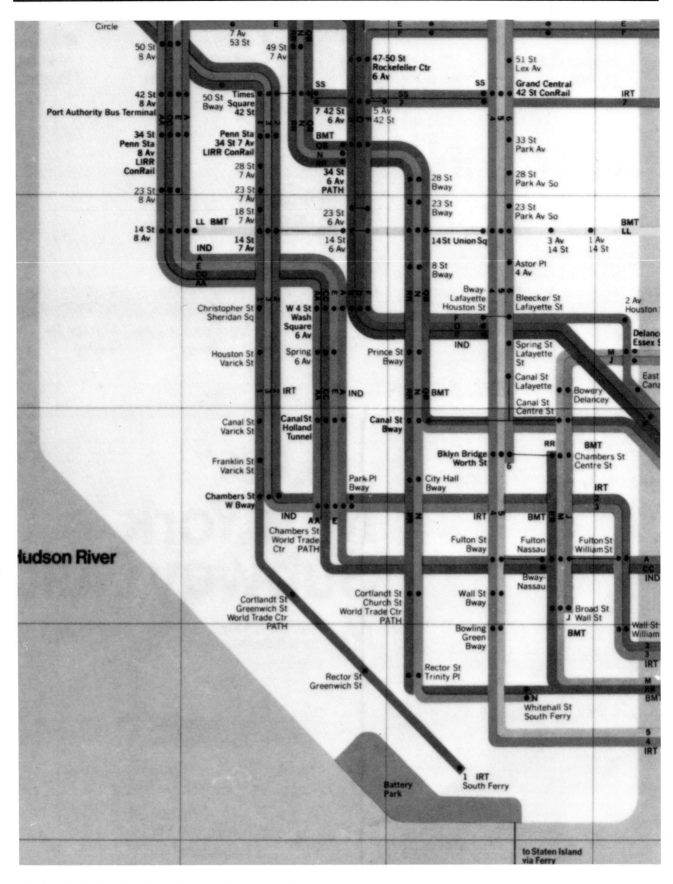

Massimo Vignelli, Detail of ''New York City Subway
Map.'' (Designer: Massimo Vignelli, Unimark International 1970)

Meaning

11

Introduction

According to writer and psychologist of art Rudolph Arnheim, works of art are "the carriers of messages about things that are not visual," things that we perceive in the world around us and within ourselves, such as tension and relaxation, rising and falling, movement and stillness. He calls these things patterns of forces or "structural themes." Most visual images don't move or change, but by arranging shape, color, texture, and other visual ingredients, artists can create visual patterns that translate these forces into a language of shape and color.

Works of visual art carry meaning through this arranging and ordering. They also can contain meaning through signs, symbols, or recognizable images of people and things, but at least part of the meaning is communicated by the way in which the forms interact. We feel the grandeur of the interior of the Pantheon (Fig. A), even though we may not know the purpose of the great Roman building. The sense of an infinity of spherical space and the titanic gesture of the dome tell us that this is holy ground. The meaning is in the forms. If a work of art tells a story we can understand *only* by recognizing the characters and associating them with information we already have, it becomes simply a vehicle for another kind of meaning.

The world is filled with teapots and lamps, posters and paintings, bridges and automobiles, many of which we might be willing to call art.

There are also many paintings and buildings, vases and sculptures, that are not art. The distinction between art and nonart is an extremely difficult one to draw. An object does not qualify as art simply because its maker *intends* it to be art. It does not become art simply as a result of the skill or training involved in its making. Most often, art is the result of a congruence or a rhyming between the way an object is conceived and the way it is made.

It "points to" a larger content through its form. The painter Henri Matisse said, "When I see the Giotto frescos at Padua, I do not trouble to recognize which scene of the life of Christ I have before me but I perceive instantly the sentiment which radiates from it and which is instinct in the composition in every line and color. The title will only serve to confirm my impression."

One theme running through the art of this century has been the effort to strip away all elements that refer to the world of things outside of the work itself and to create a "pure" work of art. The art thus produced was not necessarily popular or easily understood, but it did teach many artists and viewers to look at art differently and to be more conscious of the special way that the visual arts carry meanings.

Figure A. Giovanni Paolo Panini, "The Interior of the Pantheon." c. 1740. (National Gallery of Art, Washington; Samuel H. Kress Collection)

A

Visual Biases

Everyone has biases—habits of thinking or ways of seeing or not seeing things that are so ingrained that we fail to notice them. We could say, for instance, that to many city dwellers, all horses look alike. A horse breeder or veterinarian, however, will see differences that would never be noticed by a city person. The horse breeder's eyes are no sharper, but the breeder *is* in the habit of looking for certain details, the width of the animal's skull or the shape of the rib cage, upon which the untrained viewer would not focus attention.

What we pay attention to may also be conditioned by our surroundings. For instance, in the English language there is only one word for snow: we apply the term *snow* to any kind of frozen white stuff that falls from the sky. The Eskimos, however, have different words for soft drift snow, or the stinging needles of fine dry snow driven by wind, or the heavy wet flakes that come with relatively warm temperatures, and many other kinds that a hunter in such a climate would need to spot.

These habits of seeing, whether they come from the demands of a profession or from an environment, are learned responses. Our visual biases, the things that we look for in art and the ways that we expect it to look, are too often habits of seeing learned so long ago that we have come to think of them as natural.

When we see art from other cultures, the products of different visual biases, we sometimes fail to see the visual logic behind it. Western anthropologists were astonished to find that tribesmen in New Guinea were unable to see any resemblance between themselves and the black and white snapshots taken of them by scientists. Typically, the tribe members would point out that the photos did not look at all like the subjects because the camera image was too different from them in a number of ways: the image of a 5-foot-tall person was 2 inches tall, the image was flat rather than three dimensional, it had no back, it was colorless. To a viewer with different expectations about what to look for in a picture and what not to look for, our idea of realism looks less realistic.

Part of the value of learning about visual

A

B

forces, the language of form, lies in the fact that such a language operates in art without regard to style or the culture from which it comes. Diagonals in a design, for instance, create movement, whether that design happens to be a Baroque painting **(Fig. A)** or an Indian sculpture **(Fig. B)**. The power of the center in a visual field, the directness of the hand, and the sense of bouyancy and balance can be felt both in a piece of late twentieth-century graphic design **(Fig. C)** and in a seventeenth-century Japanese plate **(Fig. D)**.

The language of form, in other words, is free of visual or cultural biases. It is an international tongue spoken in all periods and places where art is made. Knowing how to decipher it allows us to make connections and see the common ground as well as the differences upon which visual art is based. Knowing how to speak it allows us to join the discourse as artists.

Figure A. Peter Paul Rubens, ''Rape of the Daughters of Leucippus.'' c. 1616. (Alte Pinakoteck, Munich)

Figure B. ''Siva Nataraja.'' Indian, 13th century. (The Nelson-Atkins Museum of Art, Kansas City, Mo.; Nelson Fund)

Figure C. Tandy Belew, ''All Occasions.''

Figure D. Rectangular tray. Japanese, 17th century. (Seattle Art Museum; Eugene Fuller Memorial Collection)

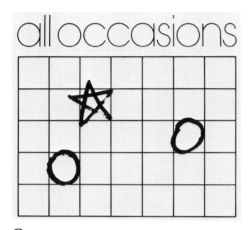

C

D

Visual Information

A central aim of visual artists has always been to take information about the visible world and put it onto a flat surface. This information might tell us about the shape of a table top, or how one tree is larger than another, or about a person standing nearby while another stands further away. A special problem with two-dimensional images is that some kinds of visual information are conveyed better by one approach than by another. For example, the subway map in **Fig. A** is not an accurate picture of the subway in the way that a photograph would be. A great deal of visual information is left out: all the small turns a train takes to go from one station to another, the tunnels, supporting beams, electrical wiring, and even the tracks. Instead the map concentrates on clearly communicating the kind of information that is

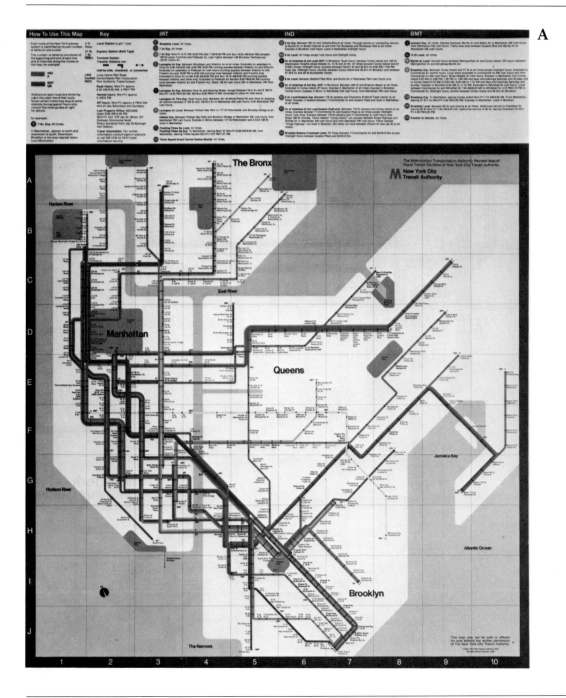

A

most pertinent to subway travelers: Which trains go to which stations? How many stops from one station to another?

One of the challenges that artists must deal with is the limited ability of a two-dimensional surface to convey certain different kinds of information simultaneously.

In the Egyptian painting of a pool **(Fig. B)** different shapes are presented—the rectangle of the pool, the almond shapes of the fishes—each in a view that most clearly conveys the characteristic shape: a "bird's-eye" view for the pool, a profile view for the fish, birds, and trees. An artist in the European realist tradition would obviously make a very different rendition of the same subject, probably something like **Fig. C**, with perspective, size changes, and other space-making devices.

For us, the Egyptian image seems unrealistic in many ways, but how does the realism of Fig. C compare? In this drawing, the shape of the pool is distorted. Rather than being a rectangle, it has four unequal sides. The trees are all wrong by Egyptian standards; some are large and some are tiny. The animals are similarly confused-looking, with different sized ducks and smudgy looking fishes. In contrast to the traditional Western aim, which is to create a world within the picture, an illusion of the depth and distance we see in the environment, the

Egyptian sees perspective and viewpoint as things that distort the "real" shape of objects. The Egyptian artist tries to show the shape of objects as they actually are "in the world out there"—the squareness of a square, the equal heights of the trees, and so on. To do this he feels free to see from any angle that will give him the clearest information. This rejection of a fixed viewpoint has its pros and cons. The clarity with which the visual information is presented is paid for with a certain sameness of vision. In Egyptian art a square is always a square, while for the Western artist the distortion of visual information permits all kinds of new and surprising shapes depending on the viewpoint. At the same time, the search for clarity has led artists to realize that what we may label "distortion" can actually be a way of dealing with the logic of the flat surface and of translating information into the language of flatness.

Also see: The Picture Plane, p. 56
Flatness & Space Together, p. 102

Figure A. Massimo Vignelli, "New York City Subway Map." (Designer: Massimo Vignelli, Unimark International 1970)
Figure B. "A Pond in a Garden." Fragment of an Egyptian wall painting. c. 1400 B.C. (Reproduced by Courtesy of the Trustees of the British Museum)

B

C

Visual Signs & Visual Symbols

A SIGN is anything that stands for anything else. The ringing of a bell may stand for lunchtime, or a fire, or the correct answer on a quiz show. A red circle displayed at a train crossing may mean that a train is coming. In drawing a map, we might use the letter *A* to stand for one location and *B* to stand for another.

Visual signs, such as the red circle or the two letters, do not have to parallel or reflect any characteristic or aspect of the things that they stand for. Shapes, colors, and other qualities of these signs are relatively arbitrary. A circle of another color could be used to indicate that the train is coming, as long as the person waiting to cross is told which colors stand for which messages.

A *symbol*, unlike a sign, is a graphic equivalent of some object, activity, or idea. For instance, the swastika was the emblem of the Nazi Party, and to us it was a *sign* that stood for fear and oppression because of its associations. The same configuration, as it was used in ancient China, was a *symbol* of change and movement: its dynamic criss-crossing and visual rotation was a visual equivalent of the mental concept **(Fig. A).**

Obviously, making a sign in the simplest sense doesn't place any great demand on the artist. Making a symbol, however, requires more thought and planning.

An interesting example of symbols is found in the thousands of characters that are used for writing the Chinese language. Developed over many thousands of years, the characters are actually pictures of the words they represent. Picture writing was, of course, used in other ancient civilizations, such as Egypt, but the Chinese characters, originally fairly realistic images, have evolved into effective graphic symbols. They combine the simplicity, legible structure, and recognizability necessary to any kind of handwriting, with a concrete image. The character for horse in **Fig. B** presents in a simplified way the flying mane and legs of a horse. Other characters also carry the visual ''memory'' of the pictures upon which they are based.

A graphic symbol can be as simple as a geometric shape or as complex as a realist portrait. A triangle might be an effective symbol for the social organization of ancient Egypt—firmly planted on a broad base of peasants, narrowing as it rises to a point which could represent the singularity, distance, and dominance of the Pharoah **(Fig. C).** Placed on an angle, with its center marked, it could be seen instead as representing equality among three subdivisions. The top of the pyramid is no longer dominant but becomes one of three equal partners whirling around a new dominant point: the center **(Fig. D).**

In general, simple geometric shape is useful in picking out a particular property from a whole constellation of forces. The *New Yorker* Magazine advertisement in **Fig. E,** through the dynamics of a straight and curved line, focuses only on the notion of balance.

The symbolism of simple geometric shape, while powerful, may also be vague or general. The context must tell us how to interpret the image. The white circle broken by the invading force of a red triangle in Lissitzky's poster **(Fig. F)** may stand for the conflict of political ideas, or it may symbolize a splitting headache. It is only

A

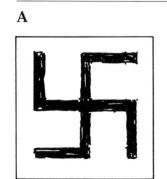

B

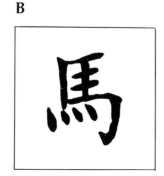

C

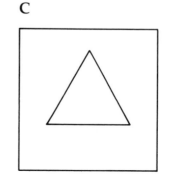

D

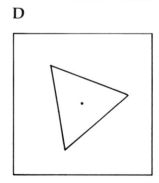

the interpretation of the text that tells us that the red stands for the revolution and not for a headache, and the white stands for an army rather than a poor head. Text transforms signs into symbols which give visual form to large and complex ideas and interactions.

Also see: Color Symbolism, p. 228

Figure E. Sven Mohr, Magazine Ad for *New Yorker* Magazine. (Sven Mohr, Lord, Geller, Federico, Einstein, New York)

Figure F. El Lissitzky, ''Beat the Whites with the Red Wedge.'' 1919. (Stedelijk van Abbemuseum, Eindhoven, the Netherlands)

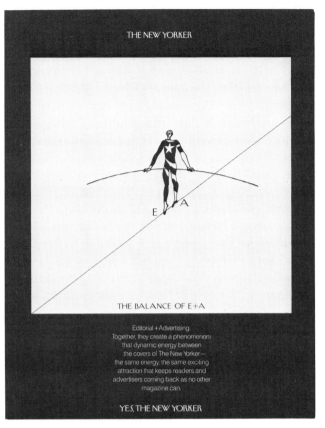

E

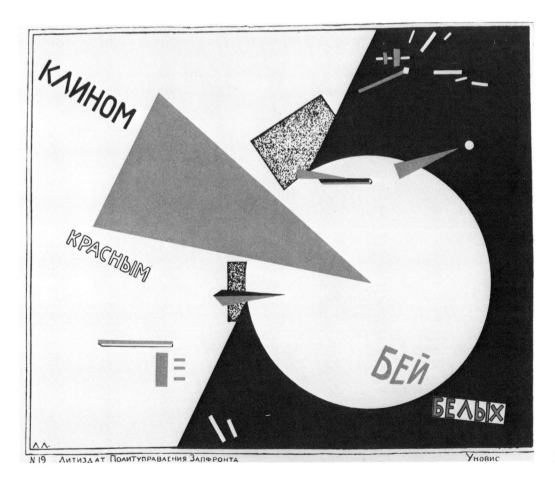

F

Realism & Abstraction

THE terms *realism* and *abstraction* have never been adequate terms to describe the range of approaches that artists have used. There are, for instance, on the one hand, artists who avoid even a hint of realistic or figurative imagery, no matter how slight **(Fig. A).** There are also artists who work directly from a model or reference point, such as a landscape or a person posing. It could be argued, though, that the first type makes an art based on reality: paint, metal, or clay treated only as physical facts, an "art of the real." A painter of landscape, in this view, deals with the opposite of reality, illusion, making a scene seem to appear from a pattern of colored tones.

Between these two hypothetical extremes, there are many artists, such as Paul Klee, or Picasso, who are neither "realists" nor "abstract" artists. There are also designers, who bring images from photography or illustration together with nonfigurative elements such as letterforms.

Realism and *abstraction* are sometimes confusing terms because they are two labels that have been used so often to describe so many different kinds of visual images that they seem almost to wilt under the burden of responsibility.

If, as we said in the introduction to this section, works of art carry messages about nonvisual things, then we might say that art is about feeling. Feeling needs form. Most people can remember, at one time or another, having an "unformed" or vague feeling or thought, and the annoying or frustrating sensation that always comes with such moments, as if we were locked in a small room with something we could not get hold of.

Artists then are form makers in that they search for content through elements such as form, color, and composition.

The various kinds of realism have a special ability to clothe disembodied feelings, natural forces, and personal insights into recognizable and tangible form. In Greek mythology, for ex-

A

B

Figure A. Kenneth Noland, ''Across.'' 1964.

Figure B. Titian, ''The Rape of Europa.'' 1559–1562. (Isabella Stewart Gardner Museum, Boston)

ample, external nature and the inner nature of people are cast into the form of people acting upon one another. Hundreds of years ago Greek myths were told so often that the characters were as totally familiar to the audience as Mickey Mouse and Donald Duck are to us. The richness and insight of the paintings, prints, or sculptures produced were often the result of the artist's long familiarity with the story and sense of authority about it.

The mature artist attempting to paint, say, the Rape of Europa, was able to conceive a personal version of the story. Titian's rendering **(Fig. B),** a late painting, clothes an elemental story of trickery and lust in carefully selected forms: an upper-class Venetian woman with sun-bleached hair, and a white bull whose challenging gaze betrays an intelligence beyond that of any barnyard animal. The white-whiskered bull seems to become a stand-in, a self-portrait of the old painter who hasn't yet lost his eye for a lively story.

Nature shows the artist how to look at art, and art, in turn, informs reality. For example, the Bible episode of the calling of St. Matthew may have suggested to the artist Caravaggio a new way of looking at the Roman peasants, priests, and working people who were all around him, and the same people gave him a way to imagine the story in concrete terms **(Fig. C).** It is no contradiction to say that an artist like Caravaggio became more imaginative and inventive *not* by trying to imagine or invent, but by selectively viewing the variety that nature presents.

Realist art is not just storytelling. For the realist artist who is more than an illustrator, the great structural themes, the forces that convey gravity, movement, interaction, and relation-

ships between visual elements all carry meaning. Just as important, these forces are embedded in *things*—people, objects, and landscapes—and doing away with the world of appearances means to giving up the essences they contain. To the realist, looking at and interrogating a model or an object is a way of trying to find out

Figure C. Michelangelo Caravaggio, ''The Calling of St. Matthew.'' c. 1592–1595. (Church of S. Luigi dei Francesi, Rome)

C

what lies behind illusionism and surface appearance.

Abstraction is often taken to mean a distancing from reality. For instance, we might say that justice is an abstract idea, which exists independent of all the possible concrete examples of jurisprudence. Or, we might say that triangularity or roundness are abstract concepts, existing apart from all triangular or round objects that we can have.

Abstraction is not a mode of escaping or opposing reality. Realism and abstract art are not at war with each other, but rather have existed side by side for thousands of years. The ''purist'' style of geometric form seen in the pyramids and obelisks of ancient Egypt coexisted with a range of refined realistic styles found in portrait, figure, and animal sculpture. In between these two extremes were numerous styles that combined accurate observation with geometry.

Whether an artist was a ''realist'' or an ''abstract artist'' was more of an issue in some places and eras than in others. Some early twentieth-century artists in Europe, for instance, felt that modernist styles such as Purism or Constructivism would make recognizable imagery old fashioned or obsolete **(Fig. A).** For many artists of this period, it seemed that museums and galleries were full of storytelling pictures illustrating history or mythology in a worn-out visual language. By comparison, abstraction seemed to offer a new visual language. Rather than asking what the subject of the picture was, or which Greek or Roman myth it illustrated, artist and viewer began to focus more on its shapes, colors, and compositional movements. The language of form and color interaction was seen as a purer language for art, not cluttered with imagery and therefore more able to express the physical, emotional, and psychological forces that we perceive around us.

This ''reeducation'' of vision made the point that all the visual configurations we make—paintings or books, furniture or tapestries, realistic or not—are governed by the same laws, affected by the same forces, and able to communicate by the same medium of visual thought.

There has also been a realization that the most important thing the visual arts must do is to be alive. The figures in a wax museum, may seem lifelike in every detail but despite the realism and skill with which they are made, lack a core of vital energy, the spark that turns the illusionistic into the real. This quality is as important in abstract art as it is in representational art.

The abstract artist deals with a subject also. People unused to looking at nonrealist art can feel intimidated by abstraction, believing that it deals with a mysterious subject beyond their understanding. Abstraction at its best, however, deals with themes that, even if they are mysterious, are things that we have all experienced: the pull of gravity, the sense of motion or of tension, the serene feeling of balance.

Many artists have opted for styles in between absolute realism and pure abstraction. Their work includes both the realist's connection to actual things and the abstract artist's vitality and expression achieved through the interaction of forms and colors alone.

Abstraction need not be divorced entirely from the world of appearances, but can *abstract from*, that is, reduce or simplify in an effort to find a core of meaning. It is in this sense that the word applies to much art that we see. This process, however, is one of reinvention or translation into a new visual language, achieving form that conveys essence without remaining true to the appearance of what we see. Cubist styles, for example, had as their subject matter specific objects, even portraits. However, these images were transformed by the artists' consciousness of the way we perceive time, motion, and change **(Fig. D).**

A perhaps more conservative deviation from absolute realism might be found in the distortion of forms, obviously closely observed, for the purpose of intensified expression. The heightened emotional atmosphere we sense in a painting by Soutine **(Fig. E)** suggests a vision of reality quite different from the cerebral calm of Cubism. Observation becomes not an objective activity in which our shared perceptions of the world are verified, but a strongly subjective one in which we are aware of the artist's reaction to the subject as much as of the subject itself.

Other artists find other ways to bridge the gap between working with images and working with such "abstract" elements as color, interval, and shape. Graphic designers often function as coordinators who bring together photographs, drawings, other specific imagery, and type, composing within a given format. Dealing with the needs of different clients, a designer may need a more flexible approach than the painter or sculptor. One design solution may consist entirely of letterforms arranged on a single-colored ground, while another may be a striking photographic image rendered in full color. Similarly, the craftsman may deal with an abstract vocabulary of given forms derived from the particular function of the object made. These forms can then be "distorted" in the direction of figuration or can have representational images applied to their surfaces **(Fig. F)**.

Ultimately, exactly where the work or style of the individual artist falls within the broad range from optical realism to pure abstraction is an entirely personal matter, not governed by history or the necessities of progress, but by the demands of function, instinct, and sensibility.

Figure D. Pablo Picasso, "Girl with a Mandolin (Fanny Tellier)." Early 1910. (Collection, The Museum of Modern Art, New York; Nelson A. Rockefeller Bequest)

Figure E. Chaim Soutine, "The Old Mill." c. 1922–1923. (Collection, The Museum of Modern Art, New York; Vladimir Horowitz and Bernard Davis Funds)

Figure F. Bronze ritual vessel. Chinese, Shang, 1528–1028 B.C. (Fogg Art Museum, Harvard University; Grenville L. Winthrop Bequest)

D

E

F

THE first and best way for students of the visual arts to learn is through looking. Before anything else, you must be prepared to use your eyes and to experience as much visual work as you can. Regular visits to museums, galleries, and exhibitions, an awareness of contemporary crafts, graphic, and industrial design in the workaday environment, and an inquiring and conscious *looking* will help you to clarify your own intentions for your work. Another important source lies in the writings of artists, critics, and visual workers. The reading list that follows contains suggestions from all of these areas.

Mechanics of Vision

The books in this section examine vision and how the eye works in a more scientific way than books written by artists or about art. The information they contain can be most useful to artists, however, and is presented in a clear, non-technical way.

GREGORY, R. L., *Eye and Brain: The Psychology of Seeing* (3rd ed.), World University Library. New York: McGraw-Hill, 1977. An entertaining and well-written introduction to some of the scientific research on perception, with some thoughts on the connections between perception and art.

——— *The Intelligent Eye.* New York: McGraw-Hill, 1970. A discussion of perception especially as it relates to three-dimensional illusions, such as stereoscopic photographs.

Perception

Perceptual studies—investigations of how the brain organizes the information gathered by the eye—are an increasingly important part of basic visual education. These books contain information on visual perception as it applies to art.

ARNHEIM, RUDOLF, *Art and Visual Perception: A Psychology of the Creative Eye, the New Version* (2nd ed., rev. and enl.). Berkeley: University of California Press. 1974. This is the classic text on perception and visual art. A densely woven and fascinating book which uses familiar examples to demonstrate why we perceive art as we do. It applies the principles of Gestalt psychology to visual art.

——— *Film as Art.* Berkeley: University of California Press, 1971. The special aesthetic requirements of film—a combination of words, images, and sound—and a discussion of the artistry of black and white films before the advent of sound. Still a timely and relevant book, written without jargon.

——— *Visual Thinking.* Berkeley: University of California Press, 1980. A collection of essays by the leading thinker in the field of Gestalt psychology and visual perception. Clearly written chapters on a range of subjects from What Abstraction Is Not to Vision in Education.

GOMBRICH, ERNST H., *Art and Illusion: A Study in the Psychology of Pictorial Representation* (2nd ed.). Bollinger Series: Vol. 35, A. W. Mellon Lecture No. 5. Princeton, NJ: Princeton University Press, 1965. Another theory of perception written by a well-known pioneer in perceptual studies. Large and well-illustrated, Gombrich's writings sketch out an interesting alternative to the writings on perception by Gestalt theorists.

ZAKIA, RICHARD, *Perception and Photography.* Rochester, NY: Light Impressions Corp., 1979. Gestalt perceptual principles are presented simply and clearly. The context is photography, but the explanations and illustrations are so good that this book will be of interest to anyone dealing with two-dimensional imagery.

Design Principles

These books combine elements of art criticism, studio practice, and theory. Some may be used as guides to useful procedures in addressing specific problems in the studio, while others focus on general approaches.

DONDIS, DONIS, A., *A Primer of Visual Literacy.* Cambridge, MA: MIT Press, 1973. A clearly laid out introduction to the grammar of visual form, presented in a compact book. Relies more on diagrams than examples from the visual arts to illustrate the text.

GOMBRICH, E. H., *The Sense of Order: A Study in the Psychology of Decorative Art.* Ithaca, NY: Cornell University Press, 1979. A study by a pioneer writer about art and perception in which the emphasis is on design and decorative arts, this large book discusses how we have thought about design in the past as well as assessing it today.

KEPES, GYORGY, *Language of Vision.* Chicago: Paul Theobald and Company, 1961. First published in 1944, this book weaves together elements of Gestalt perceptual theory, Bauhaus design, and classic European modernism to frame a methodical approach to visual education that has come to be accepted in America, as it had been for some time in Europe.

MARTINEZ, BENJAMIN and JACQUELINE BLOCK, *Perception, Design, and Practice.* Englewood Cliffs, NJ: Prentice-

Hall, Inc., 1985. A short primer on perceptual and design principles and their use in the studio. Illustrated with examples from art, architecture, and design.

PYE, DAVID, *The Nature and Aesthetics of Design*. London: Barrie and Jenkins, 1978. An expanded and updated version of David Pye's earlier small classic (*The Nature of Design*). A wide ranging intelligence surveying the spectrum of influences that shape the design process in two- and three-dimensional design. Gracefully written.

RYDER, JOHN, *The Case for Legibility*. New York: Moretus Press, 1979. A wonderful little book, barely the length of a lecture, about the value and canons of classic typography and their relevance to the new computer-aided typography.

THOMPSON, D'ARCY, *On Growth and Form* (abr. ed.), ed. John Tyler Bonner. Cambridge, England: Cambridge University Press, 1961. An interesting study of natural form as the byproduct of growth processes.

WOLFFLIN, HEINRICH, *Principles of Art History*, trans. M. D. Hottinger. New York: Dover Publications, Inc., 1950. A formal analysis of the underlying links and basic differences between classic and baroque art. Abundantly illustrated.

Color Theory

Each of these books outlines a complete theoretical system for color, its organization, interaction, physics, and use. All of these are books which have had particular pertinence to visual artists.

CHEVREUL, M. E., *The Principles of Harmony and Contrast of Colors*. New York: Van Nostrand Reinhold, 1981. This pioneering nineteenth century work was known and admired by many Impressionist and Post-Impressionist painters, among them Georges Seurat. It continues to be an influential work for artists and designers.

GOETHE, JOHANN WOLFGANG, *Theory of Colours*. Cambridge, MA: MIT Press, 1970. An early and very poetic attempt to examine color systematically by the nineteenth century poet, philosopher, and sometime painter.

ITTEN, JOHANNES, *The Art of Color*. New York: Van Nostrand Reinhold, 1973. An important teacher at the Bauhaus, Itten offers a simple but complete theory of color which includes both rationalist and more mystical approaches to color organization and meaning, as well as examples of color use in works of art.

MUNSELL, ALBERT H., *A Grammar of Color: A Basic Treatise on the Color System of Albert H. Munsell*, ed. and with an intro. by Faber Birren. New York: Van Nostrand Reinhold, 1969. Munsell's extremely thorough system of color organization and identification is still the one used by many paint, color, and printing companies.

OSTWALD, WILHEIM, *The Color Primer: A Basic Treatise on the Color System of Wilheim Ostwald*, ed. and with a foreword by Faber Birren. New York: Van Nostrand Reinhold, 1969. Another interesting and very complete attempt at organizing the many, sometimes contradictory, qualities of color into a single, comprehensive system.

Applications

These books we generally consider to be studio manuals or textbooks. Some outline a complete course of study; others may be used as general reference guides inside or outside of coursework.

ALBERS, JOSEF, *Interaction of Color*. New Haven, CT: Yale University Press, 1971. A hands-on, non-theoretical approach to color, centered on close observation of color effects and interactions (especially simultaneous contrast). A number of specific exercises are outlined, based on those Albers developed for his influential color course at Yale. This small, accessible paperback is an abridgement of a much larger work, reproducing ten of the original one hundred fifty screened plates and all of the text.

BAUMGARTNER, VICTOR, *Graphic Games: From Pattern to Composition*. Englewood Cliffs, NJ: Prentice-Hall, Inc., 1983. A series of specific exercises which use a simple grid as a point of departure from which to explore the design possibilities of repetition, variation, pattern, direction, scale, and texture.

CHEATHAM, FRANK R., JANE HART CHEATHAM, and SHERYL A. HALER, *Design Concepts and Applications*. Englewood Cliffs, NJ: Prentice-Hall, Inc., 1983. A primer of working concepts, and an examination of processes involved in design planning. Illustrated with a wealth of visual material.

ITTEN, JOHANNES, *Design and Form: The Basic Course at the Bauhaus*. New York: Reinhold, 1964. A description, outline, and history of the basic design curriculum for all students at the Bauhaus, perhaps the most influential early-modern school of design, written by one of the artists who designed and taught in the program.

LEWIS, JOHN, *Typography/Basic Principles*. New York: Reinhold, 1966. A good introduction to the history, variety, and techniques of designing with letterforms as they are used in printing.

SIDELINGER, STEPHEN J., *Color Manual*. Englewood Cliffs, NJ: Prentice-Hall, Inc., 1985. A useful studio manual outlining concepts of color vision and use, this book is based on the Munsell system of color organization and includes a good number of color plates illustrating that system. There are also exercises outlined at the end of each section.

General Histories of Art

These books outline the growth and shifts in style and emphasis of the arts. They also locate their subjects in time and place, relating them to other events and forces in the larger culture which have affected their development. These books are good places to begin, but don't replace the many volumes about specific styles, media, periods, and artists.

GERNSHEIM, HELMUT and ALISON GERNSHEIM, *The History of Photography, 1685–1914*. New York: McGraw-Hill, 1969. A large, encyclopediac, and readable history of the early days of photography, from experiments with optical devices and lenses in the seventeenth century up to the first appearances of photography in newspapers. Good explanations of the development of different processes—daguerreotype, photography on film, color, and photomechanical printing processes.

HONOUR, HUGH and JOHN FLEMING, *The Visual Arts: A History* (2nd ed.). Englewood Cliffs, NJ: Prentice-Hall, Inc., 1982. A general survey of the visual arts—painting, sculpture, architecture, and the craft areas—this book balances coverage of developments in European art from prehistory to the present with more thorough treatment of the art of non-European cultures than one usually finds. Elegantly written and enhanced by useful timelines and glossary.

MEGGS, PHILIP B., *A History of Graphic Design*. New York: Van Nostrand Reinhold, 1983. A thorough overview of the roots of graphic design, from Egypt up to the present day. In addition to examining broad trends such as the influence of Russian Constructivism or Art Nouveau, the work of particularly influential designers is examined in more detail.

NEWHALL, BEAUMONT, *The History of Photography*. New York: Museum of Modern Art, 1964. Covering the period from 1839 to the early 1960s, this book is less encyclopediac than the Gernsheim, but it offers an excellent introduction and overview.

Artists on Art

These are works by artists, writing about their own work, their general or philosophical approaches to making art, or about particular visual problems. Also included are several anthologies containing shorter writings and other statements by artists.

CHIPP, HERSCHEL B., *Theories of Modern Art: A Source Book by Artists and Critics*, contributions by Peter Selz and Joshua C. Taylor. Berkeley and Los Angeles: University of California Press, 1969. A large anthology of theoretical writings, letters, and statements by modern European and American artists, beginning with Cézanne.

DÜRER, ALBRECHT, *Of the Just Shaping of Letters*, trans. by R. T. Nichol. New York: Dover, 1965. A Renaissance artist's elegant musings on the role of proportion and geometry in the formation of beautiful letters.

HERBERT, ROBERT L., ed., *Modern Artists on Art*. Englewood Cliffs, NJ: Prentice-Hall, Inc., 1964. Ten unabridged essays by twentieth century artists such as Mondrian, Klee, Malevich, and Le Corbusier.

HOLT, ELIZABETH B., ed., *A Documentary History of Art* (2nd ed.), 3 vols. Garden City, NY: Doubleday, 1957. Available in three paperback volumes, this is a valuable anthology of theoretical writings, personal letters, reminiscences, and contracts between artists and patrons, from the Middle Ages to the nineteenth century. Introductory remarks and notes help to explain the stylistic and philosophical concerns of the artists.

KANDINSKY, WASSILY, *Concerning the Spiritual in Art*, trans. and intro. by M. T. Sadler. New York: Dover, 1977. Creator of some of the first purely abstract painting, Kandinsky as a writer on art reveals a poetic spirituality.

KLEE, PAUL, *Pedagogical Sketchbook*, trans. and intro. by Sibyl Moholy-Nagy. New York: F. A. Praeger, 1953.

———— *Paul Klee: The Thinking Eye*. New York: G. W. Wittenborn, 1964. Klee was an influential teacher at the Bauhaus. These two books are collections of notes drawn from his experience as a teaching artist. Suffused with a combination of mysticism and rigorous formalism, they offer some insight into the mind and methods of a major modern artist.

LYONS, NATHAN, ed., *Photographers on Photography*. Englewood Cliffs, NJ: Prentice-Hall, Inc., 1966. Written statements and personal views from twenty-three pioneers of photography, ranging from Peter Emerson (1899) to Minor White (1963).

NELSON, GEORGE, *Problems of Design*. New York: Whitney Library of Design, 1957. Twenty-six essays on a wide variety of subjects—Perception, Wright's Houses, Good Design, Design as Communication—by an influential American designer.

RAND, PAUL, *Thoughts on Design*. New York: Van Nostrand Reinhold, 1970. Thoughts on a number of design-related areas, from symbolism in visual communication to the role of play in design strategies, by an American graphic designer.

TSCHICHOLD, JAN, *Designing Books*, English ed. New York: Wittenborn, Schultz, Inc., 1951. Problems of and approaches to book design by one of the great book designers of the twentieth century in the classic modernist tradition.

VAN GOGH, VINCENT, *The Letters of Vincent Van Gogh*, ed. Mark Roskill. New York: Atheneum, 1967. Van Gogh's letters document not only his emotional intensity and commitment to his work, but a methodical and thoroughly sane approach to the formal disciplines of drawing, color, and composition.

BIBLIOGRAPHY

Meaning and Criticism

These books are generally works of interpretation and criticism. They examine works of art in light of the notion that art points beyond itself toward other meanings.

BACHELARD, GASTON, *The Poetics of Space*, trans. Maria Jolas, foreword by Etienne Gilson. Boston: Beacon Press, 1969. A consideration of the mystery and beauty of enclosed spaces, houses, forests, shells, rooms, and their human value, by a twentieth century philosopher.

BERGER, JOHN, *Ways of Seeing*. London: British Broadcasting Corporation and Penguin Books, 1972. A series of short essays about how art contains meaning, and how the meanings of great works of art are related to the pressures of history, consumerism, mechanical reproduction, and advertising publicity.

HESS, THOMAS B. and JOHN ASHBERY, eds., *Light in Art*. New York: Collier Books (Art News Series), 1969. Nine essays by artists and art historians examining the meaning of light in works of art ranging from those of ancient Egypt to contemporary works which use light itself as a medium.

JUNG, CARL GUSTAV, *Man and His Symbols*. New York: Doubleday, 1969. An early psychotherapist examines the existence of universal and subconscious symbols that emerge spontaneously in the art of different periods and cultures as evidence of common human hopes and fears.

LOURY, BATES, *The Visual Experience: An Introduction to Art*. Englewood Cliffs, NJ and New York: Prentice-Hall, Inc. and Harry N. Abrams, 1961. A graceful and simple introduction to how we look at and understand works of art and design linking formal organization to other kinds of meaning. Well illustrated.

PANOFSKY, ERWIN, *Meaning in the Visual Arts*. Chicago, IL: University of Chicago Press, 1983. Written by an art historian with a special interest in iconography, the study of symbols, poses, and imagery that make up a cultural tradition.

WHITE, JOHN, *The Birth and Rebirth of Pictorial Space* (2nd ed.). New York: Harper and Row, 1972. A fascinating and carefully reasoned investigation of the development of two-dimensional strategies for representing three-dimensional space, with examples drawn particularly from art of the Renaissance.

Periodicals

Periodicals are uniquely useful in that they contain information about contemporary artists that may not appear in books. Periodicals also present recent historical and critical writing.

ART IN AMERICA
ART INTERNATIONAL
ARTS

These magazines look at contemporary art from painting to environmental sculpture. They also regularly review exhibitions by contemporary artists.

COMMUNICATION ARTS
GRAPHIS
PRINT
U&LC
VISIBLE LANGUAGE

The magazines listed deal with printed visual communication and graphic design via articles on individual designers and particular problems and aspects of visual communication.

APERTURE

Contempory and historical photography.

AMERICAN CRAFT
AMERICAN CERAMICS

Contempory crafts in all media—wood, glass, metal, fiber, and clay.

DESIGN BOOK REVIEW

Excellent contemporary survey of design in all media: architecture, industrial design, crafts, decorative arts, typography, and graphic design. Also a fine ongoing source of new books on art and design history.

Acknowledgments

NORWELL Therien first encouraged us to imagine and sketch out this book. As prime mover, his advice and encouragement were with us at every stage of its development.

We received valuable advice and encouraging reactions from Professor Cynthia Cukla, Professor Pamela Lowrie, Professor Robert Morton, Professor Patrick J. Shuck, and Professor Phillip Vander Weg who read early drafts of the manuscript. A good friend and loyal transcriber, Diane Cambra of Westport, Massachusetts, typed up a clean and coherent typescript from reams of unruly notes.

We are also grateful to Kenny Beck for giving a graceful and visually lucid form to all of this. The scores of museums, galleries, and especially the artists themselves, who always did what they could to help us locate the right visual examples for the text, have our particular thanks.

As artists who teach, we have ourselves had the chance to study with committed and passionate teachers, people who took things personally and who, rather than ''choosing an idea'' to work with, were, in fact, chosen, taken over and drawn on, by their love of the arts. To them and to the memories of Frank Caldiero and Hannes Beckmann, this book is respectfully dedicated.

Benjamin Martinez
Jacqueline Block

page 13. *A.* Photo by Enell. page 14. *B.* Courtesy of China National Tourist Office. page 15. *D.* Courtesy of Hoffman-La Roche Ltd. page 17. *B.* Pablo Picasso, ''Les Demoiselles d'Avignon.'' (1907, spring). Oil on canvas, 8′ × 7′8″. Collection, The Museum of Modern Art, New York. Acquired through the Lillie P. Bliss Bequest. *C.* Courtesy of the designer. page 18. *A.* Eugène Atget, ''Magasin, avenue des Goebelins.'' 1925 PP:83. Gold-toned printing-out paper, $9\frac{3}{8}$ × 7″. Collection, The Museum of Modern Art, New York. The Abbott-Levy Collection. Partial gift of Shirley C. Burden. page 20. *A.* Lyubov Popova, ''Architectonic Painting.'' 1917. Oil on canvas, $31\frac{1}{2}$ × $38\frac{5}{8}$″. Collection, The Museum of Modern Art, New York. Philip Johnson Fund. page 21. *C.* Alexei Gan, ''First Exhibition/Contemporary Architects/ S.A.'' 1928. Letterpress, $42\frac{1}{4}$ × $27\frac{3}{4}$″. Collection, The Museum of Modern Art, New York. Gift of Alfred H. Barr, Jr. *D.* Pierre Bonnard, ''Screen.'' 1897. Lithograph, printed in color. Each panel 54 × $18\frac{3}{4}$″. Collection, The Museum of Modern Art, New York. Abby Aldrich Rockefeller Fund. page 23. *D.* Edvard Munch, ''Anxiety.'' 1896. Lithograph, printed in color, composition: $16\frac{3}{8}$ × $15\frac{3}{8}$″. Collection, The Museum of Modern Art, New York. Abby Aldrich Rockefeller Fund. *E.* Tadanori Yokoo, ''Made in Japan, Tadanori Yokoo having reached a climax at the Age of 29, I was Dead.'' 1965. Silkscreen, 43 × $31\frac{1}{8}$″. Collection, The Museum of Modern Art, New York. Gift of the artist. page 25. *C.* Copyright © 1982 by Leo Lionni. Reprinted by permission of Pantheon Books, a Division of Random House. page 27. *F.* Courtesy, Collection of Consolidated Foods Corporation. page 29. *B.* Courtesy of Robert Jensen. page 31. *B.* G. Klutsis, ''Fulfilled Plan Great Work.'' 1930. Gravure, $48\frac{5}{8}$ × 33″. Collection, The Museum of Modern Art, New York, Purchase Fund. *C.* Henri de Toulouse-Lautrec, ''Troup of Mlle. Eglantine.'' 1896. Lithograph, printed in color, composition: $24\frac{1}{8}$ × $31\frac{1}{4}$″. Collection, The Museum of Modern Art, New York. Gift of Abby Aldrich Rockefeller. page 32. *B.* Photo courtesy of the French Government Tourist Office. *C.* Courtesy Meganck Ozubko Design, Seattle. page 33. *E.* Photo courtesy of Zabriskie Gallery, New York. page 34. *C.* Hector Guimard, ''Exposition Salon du Figaro le Castel Beranger.'' 1900. Lithograph, 35 × $49\frac{1}{4}$″. Collection, The Museum of Modern Art, New York. Gift of Lillian Nassau. page 35. *D.* Photo by Bevan Davies, courtesy of Leo Castelli Gallery, New York. page 36. *B.* Gerrit Rietveld, ''Red and Blue'' Chair. c. 1918. Painted wood, $34\frac{1}{8}$ × $26\frac{1}{2}$ × $26\frac{1}{2}$″. Collection, The Museum of Modern Art, New York. Gift of Phillip Johnson. page 46. *A.* Photo by Robert E. Mates. page 47. *C.* Elizabeth Murray, ''Popeye.'' New York, 1982. Pastel on torn and pasted paper, $76\frac{1}{4}$ × $37\frac{5}{8}$″. Collection, The Museum of Modern Art, New York. Gift of Abby Aldrich Rockefeller (by exchange). page 48. *B.* Photo by Robert E. Mates. page 49. *D.* Alvin Langdon Coburn, Untitled. n.d. Plate 3 from *The Cloud.* 1912. Platinum print, $6\frac{1}{2}$ × 5″. Collection, The Museum of Modern Art, New York. Purchase. page 51. *E.* Courtesy of Dennis Thompson, Jody Thompson, Lori Wynn: The Thompson Design Group, San Francisco. page 52. *B.* Courtesy of Pentagram Design, London. page 54. *B.* Edward Weston, ''Neil, Nude.'' 1925. Platinum/palladium print, $9\frac{1}{8}$ × $5\frac{1}{2}$″. Collection, The Museum of Modern Art, New York. Purchase. © 1981 Arizona Board of Regents, Center for Creative Photography. *C.* Courtesy Frances Butler, Berkeley, Calif. page 56. *A.* Courtesy David Hockney, London. page 58. *D.* Photo by Joseph Szaszfai. page 61. *C.* Piet Zwart, '' 'Hot Spot' leiden onherroepelijk tot den DOORSLAG/Behoedt UW Kabelinet voor 'Hot Spots' door N.K.F. KABEL/NEDERLANDSCHE KABELFABRIEK DELFT (Hot Spots irrevocably lead to a blown fuse/Protect your cable network by N.K.F. cable/Dutch cable factory Delft).'' 1926. Letterpress, $9\frac{7}{8}$ × $6\frac{5}{8}$″ (25 × 16.8 cm). Collection, The Museum of Modern Art, New York. Gift of Philip Johnson. page 62. *A.* Jasper Johns, ''Between the Clock and the Bed.'' 1981. Encaustic on canvas, $6'1\frac{1}{2}$″ × $10'6\frac{5}{8}$″. Collection, The Museum of Modern Art, New York. Given anonymously. page 63. *D.* Photo by Rudolph Burckhardt, courtesy of Leo Castelli Gallery, New York. page 64. *A.* Courtesy of Massimo Vignelli, Vignelli Associates, New York. page 65. *D.* Courtesy of Herb Lubalin Study Center of Design and Typography, The Cooper Union, New York. Page 73. *F.* Will Bradley, ''The Inland Printer Christmas.'' 1895. Letterpress, $12\frac{1}{2}$ × $8\frac{1}{2}$″. Collection, The Museum of Modern Art, New York. Gift of Joseph H. Heil. *G.* Gustav Klimt, ''Hope II.'' 1907–1908. Oil and gold on canvas, $43\frac{3}{8}$ × $43\frac{3}{8}$″. Collection, The Museum of Modern Art, New York. Mr. and Mrs. Ronald S. Lauder and Helen Acheson Funds, and Serge Sabarsky. page 74. *B.* Henri de Toulouse-Lautrec, ''Jane Avril: Jardin de Paris.'' 1893. Lithograph, printed in color, composition: $48\frac{5}{8}$ × 35″. Collection, The Museum of Modern Art, New York. Gift of A. Conger Goodyear.

page 75. *C.* Laszlo Moholy-Nagy, Poster (photomontage). Photograph courtesy, The Museum of Modern Art, New York. page 79. *C.* Photo by Geoffrey Clements Photography. *D.* Bruno Munari, ''Compari.'' 1965. Offset lithograph, $77\frac{1}{4}$ × $109\frac{1}{4}$″. Collection, The Museum of Modern Art, New York. Gift of the designer. page 81. *C.* Man Ray, ''Keeps London Going.'' 1932. Offset lithograph, $39\frac{5}{8}$ × $24\frac{1}{4}$″. Collection, The Museum of Modern Art, New York. Gift of Bernard Davis. page 83. *D.* Photograph by Foto Moderna. page 85. *D.* Courtesy of John Hejduk. page 90. *B.* George Barnard, ''Ruins of a Railroad Depot, Charleston, South Carolina (1864–1865). Plate from *Photographic Views of Sherman's Campaign.* New York, 1866. Albumen-silver print from glass negative, $14\frac{3}{4}$ × $10\frac{1}{16}$″. Collection, The Museum of Modern Art, New York. Acquired by exchange. page 92. *A.* SCALA/Art Resource. page 93. *B.* Courtesy April Greiman, Inc., Los Angeles. page 94. *A.* Joseph Cornell, ''Object.'' 1942–1953. Wooden box with twenty-one compasses set into a wooden tray resting on plexiglass-topped and partitioned section, divided into seventeen compartments containing small miscellaneous objects and three-part hinged lid covered inside with parts of maps of New Guinea and Australia, $2\frac{5}{8}$ × $21\frac{1}{4}$ × $10\frac{3}{8}$″. Collection, The Museum of Modern Art, New York. Mr. and Mrs. Gerald Murphy Fund. page 95. *C.* Tina Modotti, ''Number 30/Staircase.'' c. 1923–1926. Platinum print, $7\frac{3}{16}$ × $9\frac{5}{16}$″. Collection, The Museum of Modern Art, New York. Given anonymously. *D.* Photo, The Green Studio Limited, Dublin. page 96. *A.* Courtesy of Weymouth Design, Boston. page 98. *A.* Courtesy of Ex Libris, New York. page 99. *D.* Photo by D. James Dee, courtesy of O. K. Harris Works of Art, New York. page 101. *B.* Courtesy of Katz Wheeler Design, Philadelphia. page 102. *A.* Courtesy of the artist and Robert Schoelkopf Gallery, New York. *E.* Courtesy of Katz Wheeler Design, Philadelphia. page 104. James Rosenquist, ''Fahrenheit 1982 Degrees.'' 1982. Brush and ink on frosted mylar, $33\frac{1}{4}$ × $71\frac{3}{4}$″. Collection, The Museum of Modern Art, New York. Gift of the Lauder Foundation. page 106. *B.* Courtesy of Chermayeff & Geismar Associates, New York. page 107. *D.* Courtesy of the artist and Robert Schoelkopf Gallery, New York. *E.* © Eugene Gordon 1984. page 108. *A.* Photograph courtesy of the Reinhold-Brown Gallery, New York. page 109. *D.* James Rosenquist, ''Fahrenheit 1982 Degrees.'' 1982. Brush and ink on frosted mylar, $33\frac{1}{4}$ × $71\frac{3}{4}$″. Collection, The Museum of Modern Art, New York. Gift of the Lauder Foundation. page 110. *B.* Pablo Picasso, ''Nude Seated on a Rock.'' Summer 1921. Oil on wood, $6\frac{1}{4}$ × $4\frac{5}{8}$″. Collection, The Museum of Modern Art, New York. James Thrall Soby Bequest. page 111. *C.* Winfred Gaul, ''Images Meditatives Ausstellung Gallerie St. Stephen Wien (Meditative Images).'' 1960. Silkscreen, $27\frac{5}{8}$ × $19\frac{5}{8}$″. Collection, The Museum of Modern Art, New York. Gift of the designer. *D.* Fernand Leger, ''F. Leger Museum Marsbrioch Leverkusen.'' 1955. Lithograph, 30 × $22\frac{1}{4}$″. Collection, The Museum of Modern Art, New York. Gift of Mourlot Freres. page 112. *A.* Balthus, ''The Street.'' 1933. Oil on canvas, $6'4\frac{3}{4}$″ × $7'10\frac{1}{2}$″. Collection, The Museum of Modern Art, New York. James Thrall Soby Bequest. page 113. *E.* Claes Oldenburg, ''Geometric Mouse Scale A.'' 1975. Painted steel and aluminum, $12'1\frac{1}{2}$″ × 12′6″ × $14'10\frac{1}{4}$″ overall. Collection, The Museum of Modern Art, New York. Blanchette Rockefeller Fund. page 114. *A.* Paul Klee, ''Around the Fish.'' 1926. Oil on canvas, $18\frac{3}{8}$ × $25\frac{1}{8}$″. Collection, The Museum of Modern Art, New York. Abby Aldrich Rockefeller Fund. page 121. *E.* Photo by Geoffrey Clements Photography. *F.* Leo Lionni, ''Olivetti, Lettera 22.'' 1956. Silkscreen, each $26\frac{3}{8}$ × $18\frac{3}{8}$″. Collection, The Museum of Modern Art, New York. Gift of the Olivetti Corporation. page 123. *C.* Photo by Geoffrey Clements Photography. *D.* Photo, The Green Studio Limited, Dublin. *E.* Courtesy of Frumkin Gallery, New York. page 125. *C.* Courtesy Pentagram Design Ltd., London. *E.* Pierre Matisse Gallery, New York. page 131. *C.* Kurt Schwitters, ''Merz Drawing.'' 1924. Collage of cut colored papers and a button, $7\frac{3}{4}$ × $6\frac{1}{8}$″. Collection, The Museum of Modern Art, New York. Katherine S. Dreier Bequest. page 134. Pablo Picasso, ''Sculptor at Rest before a Small Torso.'' March 30, 1933. Etching, printed in black, plate: $7\frac{5}{8}$ × $10\frac{1}{2}$″ (19.4 × 26.7 cm). Collection, The Museum of Modern Art, New York. Purchase Fund. page 138. *B.* Photo courtesy Davis and Langdale Company, Inc. page 139. *E.* Courtesy of Gilbert Associates, Providence, R.I. page 140. *A.* Photo by PMA. page 141. *B.* Photo by Robert E. Mates. page 143. *E.* Henri Matisse, ''Reclining Nude.'' 1938. Charcoal, $25\frac{3}{8}$ × $31\frac{7}{8}$″. Collection, The Museum of Modern Art, New York. Purchase. page 144. *A.* Courtesy of Information Science Incorporated. page 145. *C.* SCALA/Art Resource, New York. *D.* Photograph by Joel Breger. page 146. *B.* Lowell Williams

Design, Inc., Houston. page 147. *D.* Pablo Picasso, "Man Seated at a Table." 1914. Pencil 13 × 10". Collection, The Museum of Modern Art, New York. The John S. Newberry Collection. page 148. *A.* Pablo Picasso, "Sculptor at Rest before a Small Torso." March 30, 1933. Etching, printed in black, plate: $7\frac{5}{8} \times 10\frac{1}{2}$" (19.4 × 26.7 cm). Collection, The Museum of Modern Art, New York. Purchase Fund. page 149. *C.* Alberto Giacometti, "Portrait in an Interior." 1951. Lithographic crayon and pencil, sheet: $15\frac{3}{8} \times 10\frac{7}{8}$". Collection, The Museum of Modern Art, New York. Gift of Mr. and Mrs. Eugene Victor Thaw. page 150. *A.* Courtesy of Frumkin Gallery, New York. page 154. *A.* AP/Wide World Photos. page 155. *B.* Clarence White, "Miss Grace." c. 1898. Platinum print, $7\frac{7}{8} \times 5\frac{5}{8}$". Collection, The Museum of Modern Art, New York. Gift of Mrs. Mervyn Palmer. page 156. *A.* Jacques Henri Lartigue, "Grand Prix of the Automobile Club of France, Dieppe." 1911. Gelatin-silver print, $10 \times 13\frac{1}{2}$". Collection, The Museum of Modern Art, New York. Gift of the photographer. page 157. *E.* Jean Arp, "Squares Arranged According to the Law of Chance." 1917. Collage of cut-and-pasted color papers, gouache, ink, and bronze paint, $13\frac{1}{8}" \times 10\frac{1}{4}$". Collection, The Museum of Modern Art, New York. Gift of Philip Johnson. page 161. *C.* Frances B. Johnston, "Agriculture Mixing fertilizer" plate from an album of Hampton Institute. 1899–1900. Plantinum print, $7\frac{1}{2} \times 9\frac{1}{2}$". Collection, The Museum of Modern Art, New York. Gift of Lincoln Kirstein. page 162. *A.* Courtesy of Chermayeff & Geismar Associates, New York. *B.* El Lissitzky, "USSR Russische Ausstellung." 1929. Gravure, 49 × 35¼". Collection, The Museum of Modern Art, New York. Gift of Philip Johnson. page 164. *A.* top left. SCALA/Art Resource, New York. top right. ALINARI/Art Resource, New York. bottom left. SCALA/Art Resource, New York. bottom right. SCALA/Art Resource, New York. page 165. *B.* Courtesy of O. K. Harris Works of Art, New York. page 167. *D.* Courtesy of David Hockney. page 171. *B.* Courtesy of the photographer. page 175. *D.* Courtesy of Mary Moore. page 176. *B.* Courtesy of Davis and Langdale Company, Inc. *C.* Giorgio Morandi, "Still Life with Coffeepot." 1933. Etching, printed in black, plate: $11\frac{11}{16} \times 15\frac{3}{8}$". Collection, The Museum of Modern Art, New York. Mrs. Bertram Smith Fund. page 177. *D.* Courtesy of Jacqueline S. Casey, MIT Design Services. page 179. *C.* Courtesy of Chris Rovillo, Richards Brock Miller Mitchell and Associates, Dallas. page 181. *F.* Courtesy of James Miho and the Container Corporation of America. page 191. *D.* Photograph courtesy of the artist. *E.* Vanderbyl Design, San Francisco. page 193. *B.* Photo courtesy Jordan-Volpe Gallery, New York. page 194. *B.* Courtesy, Munsell Color, 2441 N. Calvert St., Baltimore, MD 21218. page 195.

D. Victor Moscoso, "Junior Wells and His Chicago Blues Band." 1966. Offset lithograph, $19\frac{7}{8} \times 14$". Collection, The Museum of Modern Art, New York. Gift of the designer. *E.* Henry van de Velde, "Tropon l'Aliment le Plus Concentré" (Tropon the Most Concentrated Nourishment). 1899. Offset facsimile of original lithograph, $31\frac{5}{8} \times 21\frac{3}{8}$". Collection, The Museum of Modern Art, New York. Gift of Tropon-Werke. page 197. *C.* Reprinted courtesy of Cindy M. Domínquez. page 198. *D.* Courtesy, Munsell Color, 2441 N. Calvert St., Baltimore, MD 21218. page 201. *B.* Photo by David Heald. page 207. *B.* Josef Albers, "Homage to the Square: Silent Hall." 1961. Oil on composition board, 40 × 40". Collection, The Museum of Modern Art, New York. Dr. and Mrs. Frank Stanton Fund. *C.* Photo by Carmelo Guadagno. page 210. *B.* Photo by Geoffrey Clements. page 211. *C.* Courtesy of Robert Schoelkopf Gallery, New York. *D.* Photo by Marianne Gurley. *E.* Courtesy of Robert Jensen. page 213. *B.* Courtesy Grace Borgenicht Gallery, New York. page 215. *B.* Courtesy of the photographer. *C.* Giorgio de Chirico, "The Song of Love." 1914. Oil on canvas, $28\frac{3}{4} \times 23\frac{3}{8}$". Collection, The Museum of Modern Art, New York. Nelson A. Rockefeller Bequest. page 216. *A.* Courtesy of Graham Modern Gallery, New York. page 218. *A.* Ivan Chermayeff, Chermayeff & Geismar Associates, New York. page 219. *C.* Photo courtesy of M. Knoedler & Co., Inc., New York. page 223. *B.* Jean Arp, "Enak's Tears (Terrestrial Forms)." 1917. Painted wood relief, $34 \times 23\frac{1}{8} \times 2\frac{3}{8}$". Collection, The Museum of Modern Art, New York. Benjamin Scharps and David Scharps Fund and Purchase. page 225. *C.* Richards Estes, "Double Self-Portrait." 1976. Oil on canvas, 24 × 36". Collection, The Museum of Modern Art, New York. Mr. and Mrs. Stuart M. Speiser Fund. page 228. *A.* Paul Klee, "Fire at Evening." 1929. Oil on cardboard," $13\frac{3}{8} \times 13\frac{1}{4}$". Collection, The Museum of Modern Art, New York. Mr. and Mrs. Joachim Jean Aberbach Fund. page 230. Designer: Massimo Vignelli, Unimark International, 1970. page 235. *C.* Courtesy of Tandy Belew, San Francisco. page 236. *A.* Designer: Massimo Vignelli, Unimark International, 1970. page 239. *E.* Sven Mohr, Lord, Geller, Federico, Einstein, New York. page 240. *A.* Photo by Steve Sloman, courtesy of André Emmerich Gallery, New York. page 242. *C.* SCALA/Art Resource. page 244. *D.* Pablo Picasso, "Girl with a Mandolin (Fanny Tellier)." Early 1910. Oil on canvas, $39\frac{1}{2} \times 29$". Collection, The Museum of Modern Art, New York. Nelson A. Rockefeller Bequest. page 245. *E.* Chaim Soutine, "The Old Mill." c. 1922–1923. Oil on canvas, $26\frac{1}{8} \times 32\frac{3}{8}$". Collection, The Museum of Modern Art, New York. Vladimir Horowitz and Bernard Davis Funds.

Page numbers in italics refer to illustrations.